IMAGINE
A Perfect Utopia

By "Sir Thomas More X"

For everyone who dreams of a better world...

...and so, for everyone.

ACKNOWLEDGMENTS

The author wishes to acknowledge the late Walter Earl Brown for the song "If I Can Dream" which he wrote for Elvis Presley and whose theme very aptly embodies the spirit of this book and the first stanza of which sets the tone for this book's overall message.

The author likewise wishes to acknowledge the late immortal John Lennon for his song "Imagine", the very enlightened and enlightening passages of which so succinctly identify the greatest scourges afflicting human society, and which this author had quoted freely to emphasize and lend poetic flavor to the treatment of those realities.

The author further wishes to acknowledge the many well-known people, both living and deceased, whose names, characters, experiences and stories had been mentioned and quoted to illustrate the various hypotheses, suppositions and ideas presented in this book.

TABLE OF CONTENTS

Table of Contents 2

IMAGINE

A Perfect Utopia

THE IMPOSSIBLE DREAM

"There must be lights burning brighter somewhere
Got to be birds flying higher in a sky more blue
If I can dream of a better land
Where all my brothers walk hand in hand
Tell me why, oh why, oh why can't my dream come true?"
                                        - Elvis Presley

Man, alone among the creatures of the earth, has the capacity to dream – to envision and yearn for things as they could be, or should be, or as he would want them to be.

The ultimate dream for humanity as a whole is a perfect world, what has been symbolized as Utopia.

The concept of Utopia, a society that provides every need and fulfills every desire of everyone, did not begin with Sir Thomas More. The idea, or possibly what some may believe to be simply fantasy, most probably began with the earliest human beings who first harbored thoughts that circumstances could be made better for themselves and for everyone they knew or cared for.

They could have imagined or wished that trees could be made to bear fruit all year round; the nights made less cold and dark; perhaps the animals that prey on them could become docile or totally vanish from their forest habitat, and the ones they hunt for food become less difficult to catch and kill.

Many of the dreams of our earliest ancestors have become reality in our time or even much earlier, so much so that we take them for granted and do not consider these everyday things wonderful and miraculous. But enough of seemingly impossible concepts have become realities during our lifetimes and in recent history to make us believe that we can make things better, far better, with hard work and diligent research and experimentation.

The pace of scientific and technological progress that was achieved in the twentieth century, most specially the latter half and going into the twenty-first, would be mind-boggling to people who lived in the 1800's. It is mind-boggling even to us, but we have learned to accept it, happily in most instances, with some resistance and even protest in others - but certainly no longer with incredulity..

One thing everyone realizes and accepts now is the fact that hardly anything can forever withstand change, for better or worse. But most of us are optimistic we can change the world for better, at least more often for better than for worse.

We can therefore dream of a modern and universal Utopia with greater hope of seeing it become reality than anyone before us ever did. In fact, we have a more ideal world in mind than Thomas More and our other venerable forebears had, for they existed in societies and civilizations much simpler than ours.

In the first place, More's Utopia was not a universal paradise, not one where ALL people of the world lived happily and comfortably. It was just one commonwealth or state enjoying peace and plenty because it had been so blessed geographically and because it was able to impose perfect discipline and cooperation among its people and isolate itself from possible dangers from surrounding states and peoples who would otherwise have attempted to invade it and either take away or take over its natural and man-developed resources.

No nation in the world can be so physically isolated and protected at this point in time – not only because modern weapons can fly across oceans but because the entire globe has become linked through a very complex network of economic relationships and interdependence. No country is an island now.

Given today's realities, and with our mind's eye trying to foresee as best it can the changes in human circumstances that will come in the future, we must strive for a Utopia that encompasses the entire planet and all of humanity. For no nation or people will be truly secure and able to prosper and realize their aspirations, so long as there are other nations or peoples existing in inferior situations.

There, of course, will be no lack of cynics and doomsayers who will insist that a universal Utopia is the ultimate fallacy, the mother of all pipe dreams. The perfect world is a contradiction in concepts, they would say, for the world could not be made perfect or it will not be the world that we know at all, but nirvana, or some other version of heaven. They may even insist that this is not a cynic's but a realist's point of view – that that is just the way it is, and will be, for all eternity – or until the earth, the sun, our entire galaxy all vanish into the vastness of infinity, or the finiteness of the universe.

These people may be right.

But we could not all accept that as ultimate and unassailable truth. We have to dream, and try to the very limits of our individual and collective abilities to bring about the fulfilment of our dreams. Otherwise, our species is doomed, our lives will be meaningless, or at least meaningless to those who wish to believe that mankind exists not just for today and for himself and his own brief time on earth, but to somehow make the world a little better, one generation to the next, until, well, we get as close to perfection as we can hope for.

We have to go on dreaming and trying to achieve the dream of a perfect world.

But what, really, are we trying to achieve? What is a perfect world? What is *the* perfect world?

There is an old song that tells of a textile mill worker's wish for a heaven which would be a place "where the mill was made of marble, and machines were made out of gold, where nobody ever grew tired, and nobody ever grew old."

It was such a simple concept of heaven, a heaven which embodies the worker's fondest desires, not of riches and luxury nor even a life of ease – for to him, a place "where nobody ever grew tired" working long hours in a cool marble mill, "and nobody ever grew old" as to lose his job for being too feeble, was heaven enough.

The textile mill owner, presumably, must have had a vastly different idea of heaven.

An earthly man may think that a perfect world is one where beautiful women walk around naked and go to bed with any guy who asks them, but Christian nuns and fundamentalist Muslims would probably think such a place is the devil's very own lair.

The World Trade Center in New York was the hub of global commerce and a symbol of financial strength and success for most people and nations and specially for the people and organizations that maintained offices or transacted business in the edifice that was one of the most prominent landmarks of what is arguably the most important city in the world.

But it was not a symbol of international trade and commercial interaction and cooperation in the minds of the terrorists who crashed two giant airliners into its twin towers. To those terrorists and their sympathizers in various parts of the planet, the World Trade Center was a monument to the iniquities between the modern and industrialized nations on one hand and the poor and powerless peoples like the Palestinians and the Afghans on the other. It was also the symbol of the obscene excess of wealth of the corrupt and evil infidels.

The conflicting opinions on what constitutes an ideal world, on what is good and bad for individuals and society - rather than conflicting interests which may be reconciled or bargained for - may be the biggest obstacle to realizing Utopia. How can we all work at achieving something when we cannot agree on what that something should be?

Convincing everybody, or as near to everybody as possible, on what would be best for mankind and how to achieve it appears to be an impossible task. It will be easy to say that we want everyone to be rich, but that may not be workable, and, even if it were, the ways and efforts and sacrifices needed to make it happen may not be acceptable to everyone.

Or we may think every man, woman and child must enjoy complete individual freedom and personal autonomy but there will be those who believe that the individual should have obligations to his or her community and society that take precedence over one's particular choices and inclinations. For, indeed, life for a human being does not begin and end with putting food into his mouth and a roof over his head. We have become very complex creatures with so many needs and desires and one's Paradise may not be so blissful to his neighbor.

Getting the world to agree on a common, universal ideal will be just one, just the very first, mountain that we will climb, or the first mountain we will move, if we have to – and, yes, we have to.

Before we could agree on what we want our perfect world to be, we must take stock of what the world is today – look at the things that we have to change, why we have to change them. Too, we must try to foresee, to the best of our present knowledge, the probable results of changing certain situations; for there are some things better left well enough alone – at least for the time being, until our technology and/or way of thinking are better prepared for changes. After all, what is impossible and unthinkable at one time may be a piece of cake in the future; what is taboo now may be acceptable, or even preferable, a generation hence.

THE PRESENT IMPERFECT

We all know, of course, that today, at the start of the twenty-first century, or the dawn of the third millennium, counting back to the start of the Christian Era which is the measure by which most peoples and cultures mark the passing of historic time on the planet, the world is plagued by extreme inequalities among nations rich and poor, as well as individuals within each nation, rich or poor, that are at the opposite ends of the economic scale.

That is only the macro view, the simplest and quickest way to classify and describe the variations in the existence and conditions of societies and the human beings that comprise them.

There are other, almost equally vital, differences: like in the aspects of literacy and education, health, opportunity, culture, religion, even physical characteristics.

Within the main divisions that comprise the differences of such aspects of human nature and circumstance there are still many subdivisions, sometimes in such polar opposition to each other that they almost seem to belong each to different groups, instead of being parts of the same main body: for instance, in the beliefs of respective followers of the various Christian sects and in the culture and practices of some African tribes that live among each other.

When the differences are either cultural or intellectual and emotional, they are not permanent or eternal differences. They may run deep and strong for a certain time but can also crumble and disappear in one generation or after a dramatic event, like the spontaneous joining of various factions as well as ordinary citizens in the Soviet Union during the showdown between Premier Mikhail Gorbachev and other officials of his own government in 1991 which led to the sudden collapse and disintegration of the Russian-led communist federation and its strictly-controlled socialist way of life.

It may be an ironic twist of fate that the debacle of those who went against Gorbachev did not result in a triumph for him but for Russian president Boris Yeltsin, but that is beside the point – the main point is that a sea change was effected by a relatively small event in a very brief moment in history.

It may seem like all the other differences and inequalities among individuals, peoples, societies and nations will have to be set aside while economic disparity is being tackled. Economic disparity is the single most important obstacle to be overcome, for no society or individual can find contentment and happiness unless material needs are provided for, sufficiently at least, and abundantly if possible.

But then again, some of the problems may have to be addressed first before economic equality can be attained. Material abundance, after all, is dependent on so many factors. Let us, therefore, look closely and hard at mankind's most prevalent problems and try to pinpoint their causes so we can seek or devise solutions to them and eventually achieve our ultimate goal.

POVERTY: SOCIETY'S CURSE, CIVILIZATION'S BEDROCK

This could be the supreme irony of human existence. Whereas the march of civilization is supposed to be directed at improving the lives and conditions of peoples and communities striving for social, economic, technological and scientific progress, all advances thus far in the economic field had been achieved through the exploitation or utilization of some lower classes of people, either from other societies that were subdued and enslaved or from the indigenous members of the particular civilized societies that are at the lower rungs of the economic pyramid, or from unequal trade which is usually perpetuated for years and even generations.

Always, there has been the equivalent of worker ants or worker bees to provide for the needs of the colony. That situation may seem like a matter of course, the simple operation of the principle of division of labor, but then if the principle is working efficiently and logically there should be a corresponding equitable division of the fruits of labor.

The opposite is true practically everywhere and ever since human beings formed a modern community.

The farmers who plant and harvest the food crops and raise the livestock do not enjoy the most sumptuous dinner table. Except for the farmers from industrialized nations, people in this class usually have to subsist on the barest of fares. The carpenters and construction workers do not live in the grandest houses; in many third-world countries they do not even have decent living quarters beyond hovels and shacks.

To think that these are the people whose labors make it possible for everyone else to survive and exist in a level fit for humans in a civilized world.

The basic structure of all societies is in the form of a pyramid. The largest component is the base made up of the poorest members, with the pyramid slowly tapering upwards as the economic status goes higher until the pyramid is reduced to the very small point at the top. This model is the same for the world's community of nations, with only a very few super-rich countries lording it over the rest of the planet.

The citizens of the rich nations, even most of their poor, naturally enjoy a standard of living that is far above that of the poor of the impoverished countries and which would be considered affluent based on the standards of the latter. But that is relative and the poor of the rich nations are better off because the poor of the truly destitute countries are, in fact, suffering for them.

The fact that the poor or ordinary citizens of an affluent society or nation often have better living conditions than those of less successful societies or nations, because the poor and ordinary citizens of the latter do the suffering for the former, is easily illustrated by the enslavement of vanquished peoples by their conquerors in ancient times. The enslaved peoples were made to do the hard labor while being recompensed, nay, maintained, with just enough nourishment to keep them functioning.

On a higher level, Babylon, Rome and all those other empires rose to glory and maintained their grandeur through the tributes of their vassal kings, who themselves also exacted from their subjects tithes and forced labor.

In the modern age, there are no longer vassal states that pay tribute to emperors but wealthy industrialized countries dominate international trade and suck away the lifeblood of the underdeveloped nations in trade imbalances and some unfair practices like subsidizing certain industries to crush competition from those countries that could not afford subsidies for their own vital industries.

There are no longer true slaves but migrant workers who endure being away from their loved ones, their compatriots and familiar environments to do the hard work that the citizens of the affluent countries cannot or do not want to perform. Those citizens are mostly assured of some sort of welfare compensation even if they did not work, so why should they perform humble, demeaning tasks? What is more, the migrant workers, both legal and illegal, but more specially the illegal ones, are willing to accept less compensation, often far less than stipulated by the local labor laws, since even under those conditions they get much more than they would have gotten back in their homelands.

Multinational companies also exploit the cheaper labor in underdeveloped countries by moving their plants and factories to those places.

Though leaders of nations, governments and cause-oriented institutions, including religious organizations, relentlessly attempt, or profess to relentlessly attempt, to eradicate poverty and economic suffering for the masses of poor people all over the world, none of them have really succeeded, nor could any one ever hope to – not in the present system of economic and material intercourse between individual human beings, classes and states.

True, there are some, even many, poor individuals who manage to improve their lot and even rise to the very top economic stratum. But that does not really translate into a decrease of poor people or degree of poverty spread out among the members of society. For as some poor individuals become rich, so do some rich people find themselves losing some or even all of their wealth for some reason or another.

When erstwhile poor individuals manage to clamber up the economic pyramid they invariably do so by pulling down others. They become rich by taking away some of the wealth of already rich people, sometimes to the extent that some of the latter become themselves impoverished and take the former place of the new members of the "haves". Or the erstwhile poor take even more away from the already meager share of their kind to accumulate a fortune.

A laborer wants to improve his situation, he may decide to work beyond regular hours so that he gets paid more. He gains, but he also takes away the wages that would have gone to other laborers who would have done the work he did in his extra work hours. Or he will try to take over the role of his employer, perhaps by saving as much as he can of his wages until he has some capital to strike out on his own or by finding somebody to loan him the money he needs – and eventually snatch away some of the income of, or even supplant, his former employer.

An entrepreneur wishes to make more money from his enterprise, he studies the systems and manner of operation of his more successful competitors and either imitates them or devises his own better ways to counter the competition's erstwhile effective formula.

A singer wants to sell more records, he tries to sing better, or write better songs or have better songs written for him. Or have a brilliant marketing outfit handle the distribution of his records. When his record becomes a hit, the windfall did not come from heaven or materialize from thin air, as if the money he piles up would not have gone to somebody else if he did not produce that winning song or album. Either another singer or several singers would have sold records instead, or the record buyers might have spent their money on other sorts of things, through which other people or entities would have gained – but no longer, as our singer has already taken the funds to his bank.

Japan, devastated after the Second World War, rose from the ashes by imitating and then equaling or even beating technological and industrial giants like the United States, Germany and Britain. The prosperity enjoyed by the Japanese a generation after Hiroshima and Nagasaki did not spring out of Tokyo but as a result of grabbing chunks of the market shares of General Electric, Volkswagen, etc. – resulting, of course, in lighter pocketbooks for the citizens of the countries where those erstwhile industrial giants were based.

The oil-producing Arabian states increased their wealth as well as geopolitical influence by an even more direct route – jacking up the price of their oil after they have nationalized the outfits drilling the all-important commodity and from then on keeping the rest of the world on tenterhooks since they can send economies tumbling and spinning anytime they decide to increase prices or slow down their production.

The OPEC countries naturally, and probably correctly, believe that they only took what was rightfully theirs with their actions as an international oil cartel but the fact remains that the billions, nay, trillions that have been pouring into their coffers since 1973 have caused rich countries to tighten their belts and poor ones to lag further in the marathon race for development.

So much for the problems brought about by the existence of poverty and the seemingly endless and futile struggle to eradicate it from civilized human society. Let us look at the blessings, yes, blessings, that poverty has brought to humankind and civilization.

In the first place, poverty or some sort of lesser status of certain individuals in a group of humans caused the organization of tribes and then communities and ever bigger social groups. For the inferior state of some individuals caused them to accept the establishment of a hierarchy and the ascendancy of leaders.

The acceptance of a lower status by those individuals also facilitated the division of labor that made communal life more efficient and rationalized. The technological and social development of mankind was made possible by the existence of that pyramid and this fact is very evident up to the present.

What city or community could function without people to dispose of the garbage, clean and maintain the sewers, handle all the messy and lowly tasks so vital to a civilized existence?

Since the earliest days of civilization, how could progress have been achieved without farmers to produce food, laborers to build public works?

When we talk of economic disparity we think of the businessmen and owners of capital and the ruling class. These are the people who rake in the huge profits from the blood and sweat of the peasantry, so to speak. But then the peasants, or the working class, and the entire community as a whole, need them – those hated big shots.

Who will the workers work for if nobody puts up the capital for factories and industrial establishments? Can a carpenter find regular work if he were to knock on door after door asking if somebody needs a new house or wants one remodeled or repaired? Where will a printing machine operator learn his skill and then practice it if no one put up a printing company? What will a mechanic do if old Henry Ford and his colleagues did not crank out automobiles?

Then, how would society exist if there were no tough or smart guys to run city hall and the White House?

So it is a matter of both capitalists and the ruling class on the one hand, and the lowly workers on the other, needing one another. The problem is that they do not benefit equally from their symbiotic relationship.

We all know that in most countries, with the exception of the highly developed ones like the USA, Great Britain, France, Japan, Germany and Canada, the people who do the most important things – like farmers, fishermen, construction workers and waste disposal staff – are at the bottom of the social and economic pyramid.

When a nation becomes so prosperous as to be able to offer generous compensation to the lowliest workers, their erstwhile poor citizens who used to fill those roles eventually manage to raise themselves to a higher level. With the loss or reduction of that nation's poor, they have to find surrogate poor to perform the dirty work. That is why there are so many migrant workers in the developed countries, people who came from the underdeveloped regions.

It may be posited that the time may come when most, possibly even all, nations and economies in the world will develop and prosper so that everyone can live comfortably.

Logic dictates that that cannot happen. Most specially not under the current circumstances prevailing in international economics. The wealthy nations will not stand or sit idly by the wayside while the poor ones are playing catch up.

They will simply jack up the prices of commodities and products that they produce or control which the poorer countries need, or they will institute ever tougher standards to the entry of products in the market such that they will still have the lion's share. Or they will at least strive to improve their products such that they will always have a decisive edge in the free market, which they could very well accomplish with their superior resources and more advanced technology.

The rich states are not being selfish should they do these things and more to maintain their advantage in international trade. They have to do it for survival and self-preservation. For, as had been illustrated earlier, poor nations, like poor people, can only improve their lot by grabbing off from the rich ones' share of the pie.

We all accept, of course, that rich individuals and classes, as well as nations, will have to exert their utmost efforts to remain rich and even grow richer; even if it means keeping the poor poor or making them even poorer. Under the present state of things, that would seem the sensible and more beneficial thing to do.

If the poor ceased to be poor they would no longer do what poor people do. They would not plant crops, build roads, take charge of all the dirty work. The whole system of civilization would go kaput. Everybody would have to look after his own basic needs, tend a vegetable garden, pick berries in the woods, try to trap some stupid animal for meat, hack down some trees for a dwelling.

Had there been no farmers to sow crops and lowly workers to do other menial work, Michelangelo would have had to do all the things vital for his own daily survival and he would never have gotten to doing the Sistine Chapel, or Pieta or David. Galileo would have been too tired from working a small farm and could not have found time to tinker with his telescope and gaze at the heavens night after night.

Sir Isaac Newton would have been tending sheep instead of pondering the fall of an apple and Charles Darwin would have been working a mill, if somebody got around to inventing such a device at all. Everyone that ever lived would have been so preoccupied providing for his or her own needs, most likely in very primitive ways, that we could not have harnessed electricity, discovered penicillin, let alone sent men to the moon. Bill Gates would not be counting billions and nobody will be thinking of Windows other than as openings we look out of and close against the wind and the rain.

Poverty, without a doubt, is a most vital and integral pillar of civilization. The existence of inequalities in society had been the single most basic cause why man was able to achieve technological, intellectual and social progress. But we cannot perpetuate the existence of poverty or condemn the poor peoples to stagnate in their condition, nor would they themselves cease to struggle to break free from their sad state.

There has to be a way.

KINGS, PRESIDENTS AND TYRANTS: NECESSARY EVILS

Since the earliest forms of organized society, there have been leaders in one form or another – from clan elders and tribal chiefs, then later to kings and emperors and, in modern times, presidents and prime ministers. No organization or group can exist without somebody to take control and enforce order. A society of equals, without a definite someone in command, will be one of total chaos and multi-lateral conflict.

This is a fact of life even in animal societies. Elephant families have matriarchs to lead and make decisions for the entire group, horse herds have stallions looking out for their welfare and choosing where they should go. There are alpha wolves who rule the pack, silverbacks exercise command in gorilla families, and a pecking order establishes rank in many gregarious bird and mammal species.

Unlike leaders of animal groups, however, humans who hold power have always been prone to either abuse of their position and greed for more power and material gain made possible by that power, or to perpetuate the position for their progeny and kin even if these are not worthy of such. Then again, there have also been pretenders and ambitious claimants to thrones and high positions who succeeded in grabbing power even if they were no better or less deserving than those they replaced.

Unlike in animal society, where the leader or top dog is invariably deposed by a bigger, stronger and quicker, therefore better, rival, humans who hold power are not necessarily the best suited for the job; sometimes they are not even the least bit qualified for it. Or they may have wanted and held on to the position for the wrong reasons – like personal aggrandizement and material greed – instead of the only true justification for leadership, which is to protect and nurture the group or society the leader governs. The ascension to power of the undeserving was made possible by man's use of weapons, as well as deceit and unholy alliances, all of which do not exist among supposedly lowlier, but apparently nobler, creatures.

In ancient times, the removal of kings almost always entailed violence and bloodshed. In countless instances, blood relations were no hindrance to murderous conflict - brother against brother or even sister, son against father, mother against son, the quest for power was the end all and be all.

Often, when rival factions were so equally matched that no one could subdue the opposition, kingdoms and nations became split and divided. But that, of course, did not mean the end of power struggles, for rivalries within each new kingdom or nation always arose.

As more and more of the peoples of various nations became more educated and aware of the affairs of state, monarchs could no longer just hold on to power and exercise it as they wished. They had to be accountable for most of their deeds. In many cases, as a check against abusive and disastrous acts, they had to share some of their power, with councils of elders, senates, etc.

There have been, of course, countless instances when the monarchs who shared power with a group of some sort or another got them to accede to the monarchs' wishes – through bribery, collusion in running state matters, or coercion of some sort. Whatever the form of government, there was always room for misuse and abuse of power. And such, more often than not, was inflicted upon so many nations and peoples throughout history.

Democracy - the participation of the governed either in the choice of their leaders or in the manner they are governed or both, with the people at large theoretically holding the supreme authority – came about and spread around the world, bringing down the established order of hereditary rule. It has brought many welcome changes to the matter of choosing and empowering leaders and governments but it is still far from being a perfect solution.

Elections in many countries, particularly the less technologically and culturally advanced ones, are often rigged and manipulated. Throughout recent history, leaders who get the support of their country's military, or the military leaders themselves, either become dictators and virtual monarchs or change the law to perpetuate themselves in power, "legally", so to speak.

True, a leader who got or kept himself in power through dubious means may actually have his people's best interests at heart, and only employed unconventional measures to gain authority so he can do what is good for his country. But then, he may have to use other and more unconventional acts to retain the support of the sectors (i.e., the military and powerful warlords or regional and sectoral leaders) that prop him in his position. The tendency for abuse in such situations is always strong and had, in historical experience, gained the upper hand.

What about the duly elected leaders who did not cheat nor cling on to their positions beyond the tenure to which they were legally entitled? Or even resisted the temptation to remain in power legally and righteously, like Nelson Mandela of South Africa who did not seek a second term as president even though he would have surely won?

Certainly, there must be more of this type of statesman. Could we not just find ways to ensure that such leaders are the rule and the world's nations and peoples will be largely in good hands?

Unfortunately, this is a Pollyanna fantasy. Even the president of the United States of America, the icon of modern-day democracy, could hardly be said to be elected by the simple free will of the American people.

In this day and age, running for election to the presidency of the most powerful and richest country in the world is nothing like standing on an empty apple crate and talking before a crowd, then taking a train or stagecoach to the next town to do the same thing all over again, as in the days of Abraham Lincoln.

Today, even candidates for mayors of cities and state senate posts bombard the voters with television ads, and hire expensive spin doctors to run professionally-managed image projection campaigns, as well as demolition jobs on the opposition. Any candidate who hopes to have winning chances will have to spend a lot of money, most specially if he aims for the US presidency.

How many candidates have the kind of personal money – hundreds of millions, perhaps even a couple of billion dollars – to wage an honest-to-goodness presidential campaign? And if they had that, would they spend it to get into the White House? Will they throw away what should be their children's inheritance in a presidential election?

Only someone like Ross Perot could, and would, squander so many millions of his own funds to try to win the US presidency. And then he would not win - no, never.

Sure, he got 19 percent of the vote in 1992, but that was because nobody took him seriously. If Perot or somebody like him, who is running independently of the two entrenched political parties, would loom as a serious threat in a future US presidential contest, you can bet every dollar you have that giant concerns and many powerful unseen forces would gang up on him, spend staggering amounts on negative propaganda and other political tools, to prevent him from winning.

In this era of big business and conglomerate interests, of global and multinational industrial giants, no US presidential candidate could hope to win without the support of financial and industrial moguls, the so-called kingmakers. A candidate may choose not to take campaign contributions from them but he sure would not like the big shots using their money, power and influence to discredit him or boost his opponent's stock. He has to make compromises somehow somewhere.

What's more, even members of his own party would not support him if they are not assured of his own support, in some form or another, in return once he gets elected. And getting elected takes a lot of doing, not just by the candidate or his campaign staff, but by so many sectors throughout the country.

Truth is, even getting elected to town positions already entails promises and compromises that could not exactly be made known to the voters. One running for sheriff may have to assure operators of sleazy joints that he would go easy on them if elected, or a candidate for mayor may promise to take the side of land developers in his town against conservationists seeking to protect woodland habitats of endangered animal species.

It is practically impossible to find a leader who would do what is right and is best each and every time. Definitely not somebody who had to win his position with the support of so many groups and individuals, groups and individuals who have their own respective interests and concerns to protect and further and, thus, particular reasons for their support.

The only leader who could really do what he or she thinks is right and best is somebody who is not beholden to anyone for the position – like a monarch who ascended the throne by right of birth. And we have already seen how dangerous and cumbersome monarchies are. Furthermore, monarchs often had to ally themselves with, and thus had become beholden to, vassals and warlords in their kingdom to keep their thrones.

Is there, therefore, no hope for the world's nations and societies on the matter of being assured of righteous and benevolent governance?

There is. In fact, I believe I may have found the answer.

But let us not rush into that. Be patient for a while. Just read on.

WAR AND CONFLICT BETWEEN NATIONS AND PEOPLES

Throughout history, and even from prehistory, wars have been the most devastating and tragic events in human society. True, there have been disasters like the bubonic plague, as well as earthquakes, storms and floods, and eruptions of volcanoes like Vesuvius, that wreaked death and suffering on large numbers of people, but these were natural calamities, not manmade.

Wars have obliterated not only kingdoms and national boundaries, but also entire races and cultures. In so many instances, war was waged for wrong reasons, the flimsiest of reasons, or no justifiable reason at all.

How do you defend wars of conquest like Alexander the Great waged on kingdoms so far from his own Macedonia and Greece? He waged war only for the sake of subduing other kings and peoples, like a gunfighter desiring to add notches to his gun butt. The same thing goes for Genghis Khan and Napoleon Bonaparte, all those legendary conquerors who seem like heroes in history books but who were, in reality, mostly bloodthirsty megalomaniacs.

The waves of conquests, wars and pillage have deprived all mankind of the fullest glory of Egyptian culture, the wonders of Mesopotamia, Solomon's temple and the ark of the covenant, many of the treasures of ancient China, even entire civilizations like those of the Aztec and the Inca.

In many instances, wars have been waged out of greed for the riches and resources of neighboring kingdoms but which riches and resources, when won through armed conflict, had to be spent and depleted in trying to defend and keep the very same things, and to prevent the newly conquered peoples from rebelling and regaining their land and possessions.

There have also been wars brought about by differences in religious beliefs. With high priests sharing power and collaborating with monarchs - sometimes monarchs were even either high priests themselves or proclaimed as deities - there often was pressure to prove the truth and potency of their gods' power on the battlefield. So many wars were "holy" and the victors either imposed their faith on the vanquished or slaughtered those who would not be converted.

"Holy wars" will, however, be discussed more extensively in the next chapter where they more properly belong.

Sometimes, war was a political instrument that served both internal and external purposes.

When monarchs had potential rivals they sometimes waged war on another kingdom to force the rivals to pledge loyalty and help fight the war or be branded as traitors and executed or exiled and thus get severed from the mainstream of the kingdom before they were strong enough to challenge the crown. Or war is waged on another kingdom not because that kingdom posed any threat but because a monarch wished to intimidate a third kingdom.

The Iliad tells how a bitter war was fought because of one woman, Helen of Troy, and though this may be simple legend, it is not unimaginable that something of the sort has happened in the long forgotten past, since there are similar legends in Indian and other cultures.

In modern times, the sense of cultural and racial identity that had united various peoples in ancient times had evolved into a double-edged sword called nationalism. Nationalism, on one hand, is, of course, good among the people involved, as it brings them together and provides impetus for cooperation and concerted action for their common good. But it has another aspect that is very negative although hardly anyone, or at least anyone of stature and importance on the world stage, recognizes or speaks of it: that is that nationalism is divisive of the world as a whole – for while it unites a certain group of people, nationalism also separates that group from the rest of the world.

In many cases, nationalism has ignited violent conflicts, some of them quite unexpected and unthinkable just a short period before they broke out. Examples of such are the Yugoslav wars of the 1990s.

Yugoslavia, initially a kingdom formed after World War I out of mostly South Slavic people under several different suzerainties that struggled under various empires and fought different invaders, experienced a terrible trial by fire when the Germans invaded it in World War II.

The Axis allies - Germany, Italy, Hungary and Bulgaria - invaded the young nation and each occupied large areas and proceeded to eliminate Serbs, Jews, Gypsies and other ethnic groups, obviously intent on eventually claiming the territories and supplanting the populations with their own peoples.

The genocidal practices galvanized the erstwhile fragmented citizens of the different principalities that were brought together under the Kingdom of Yugoslavia. They waged fierce and valiant guerrilla warfare under the leadership of Josip Broz, whose communist Partisans eventually succeeded in driving away most of the occupying forces even before the Germans surrendered to the Allies.

Transformed into a communist republic after the war, Yugoslavia, with Josip Broz Tito (he added the last name, his codename while an underground Communist Party member, sources say) managed to forge a viable relationship between and among the member states: Serbia, Bosnia and Herzegovina, Macedonia, Montenegro, Croatia and Slovenia.

The federal government discouraged and sometimes even directly suppressed nationalistic tendencies within the states as well as ethnic groupings and thus succeeded in bringing about cooperation and coexistence that resulted in general public order and political stability. The Yugoslav nation became so politically strong that Tito was able to distance his country and eventually dissociate it from the Soviet Union, the only communist country other than China to do so.

Yugoslavs enjoyed the most freedom among all communist/socialist societies. They could freely travel and work abroad and Yugoslavia required no visas from visiting foreigners.

There was peace and a growing sense of Yugoslavian identity.

Tito was quoted as saying: "No one questioned who is a Serb, who is a Croat, who is a Muslim (Muslim was a quasi-nationality identification of Slavic Muslims living in Bosnia). We were all one people back then (referring to the wartime struggle), and I still think it is that way today."

But they were only one people under Tito's able, inspired, albeit stronghanded leadership. Tito died in 1980 and the presidency, which had been held by him as president for life, became a collective affair with each republic participating. The federal government became difficult to control even as nationalistic tendencies surfaced and smoldered.

A decade after Tito's death, nationalism - which had erstwhile been considered a political crime that endangered Yugoslavia's national policy of Brotherhood and Unity - had split Yugoslavia into seven states: Bosnia-Herzegovina, Croatia, Kosovo, Macedonia, Montenegro, Serbia and Slovenia.

Not only was Yugoslavia dismembered, the newly-independent states became engaged in wars between themselves in the 1990s and it took the intervention of the North Atlantic Treaty Organization (NATO) and other nations, with direct military action, to put an end to some of the most gruesome atrocities, mass rapes of women and genocidal purges of the late twentieth century.

Despite an internationally-brokered and UN-enforced peace in Bosnia-Herzegovina, which was the battleground in the

Yugoslav wars from 1992-95, hostilities broke out in another part of the former Yugoslavian territory – this time in the autonomous province of Kosovo – in 1998. Again, it took NATO bombing attacks and the threat of ground troop occupation to force peace.

War crimes, including ethnic cleansing and crimes against humanity, were charged against many officials and personnel from all sides of the various conflicts in the former Yugoslav nation. Many have already been convicted and many more are still on trial.

Meanwhile, the wars that were ignited by nationalism of the different ethnic and cultural components of the former Yugoslavia have left the newly independent states economically crippled and most of their population physically and emotionally damaged and traumatized.

The breakup of the Soviet Union also resulted in violence among and within many of the 15 states that arose as independent entities in the former territory of the communist empire. Nationalism, as often is the case, among the former soviet socialist republics was driven by ethnicity and, where the population of the state was of mixed ethnicity, internal conflicts naturally arose when one ethnic group dominated or tried to dominate over the others.

Where the population was largely homogeneous, conflict with the neighbors was often caused by the inequality of natural resources, industrial infrastructure and economic viability. Whereas all these were not the exclusive dominion of any one of them under the centralized rule of the

USSR, they became bones of violent contention for the now-independent and self-supporting states.

The same situation became cause for armed strife among ethnic groups sharing the same state when one group wanted to separate itself along with the territory where they are the majority and such territory happened to have better resources, which naturally could not be accepted by other groups.

There have been reports of many thousands of casualties in conflicts in the Central Asian states of the former Soviet Union but the press in those countries are still mostly government-controlled or suppressed, as they have been under the Soviet regime.

Too, they are not usually covered by international news media as they are not of great importance on the world stage. They are also far from centers of modern media, unlike Yugoslavia which is bounded by affluent European nations.

Further, the Western press seems to be fixated on the perception that the breakup of the Soviet Union is a great blessing for the entire world – good for the members of the USSR and everybody else – and turn a blind eye on, or belittle the rumblings and cries from, the remote states.

Nevertheless, we know that sporadic violent confrontations have broken out and are still taking place in Chechnya, Georgia, South Ossetia, Abkhazia and Transdniestria.

In many places in Africa, the nations that were granted independence from colonial powers and many that were formed by various political movements have mostly suffered for decades because of ethnic differences and struggles to gain power or a separate state for different tribes.

There had been peace in the Dark Continent before Great Britain, France, Belgium and the Netherlands found the colonies too cumbersome and no longer in their best interests to maintain. Of course, in colonial times, the African peoples were kept in virtual bondage as they mostly remained peasants and the talented few who became educated mostly served in the colonial governments and the vast majority lived and died in poverty. But the lot of most present-day Africans cannot be said to be any better. They are worse off, with thousands dying of hunger, disease, direct war violence and atrocities; and those still surviving are living in constant fear and with hardly any hope for a better life.

The struggle for national freedom, and even the attainment of it, is a continuing cause for people to suffer and inflict suffering on others.

The late musical legend John Lennon's most memorable song "Imagine", which is regarded as his personal anthem, and in which he apparently was able to summarize the greatest problems of humanity, has the following second stanza:

"Imagine there's no countries
It isn't hard to do
Nothing to kill or die for..."

Surely, the countless experiences throughout history and the bitter and gruesome lessons from two world wars and more than a dozen smaller-scale but no less brutal hostilities ought to have impressed on the minds of all thinking men, particularly leaders of nations, the utter inhumanity and severe cost in lives, emotions and, yes, national economies of engaging in such confrontations.

Too, with all the advances in technology, philosophy and the social and political sciences, besides the birth and rise of humanist thinking, one would expect that senseless violence and armed conflict would be a thing of the past in the modern world.

But it ain't so.

Man continues to fight and kill his fellows even when it is obvious that violence will not solve the problem, unless the other side is completely annihilated, which may no longer happen unless nuclear, biological and other hideous weapons are employed.

The cannonballs keep flying. Men and women, children and their friends keep dying.

GOD: ONE MORE NECESSARY EVIL

Most people who have religious faiths and convictions consider their respective beliefs as the most essential pillar, the lynchpin, of their lives and existence – and even, in fact, the existence of the entire universe.

The followers of every sort of faith believe themselves to be created and existing either as part of the grand design of a supreme being or beings, or created to prove themselves worthy of the deity's blessings including, in many religions, the gift of eternal life.

That may seem harmless, even beneficial, for the peace of mind and temporal guidance of the faithful. The problem, however, lies in the fact that every religion arrogates unto itself sole possession of the Truth. Almost every religion declares itself as the only way to paradise and eternal life.

Most people do not realize or recognize the untold sufferings brought upon humanity by the existence of such beliefs.

How many people have been tortured and killed for not believing as the rest of the community, or at least the powerful in the community, did – as in the Inquisition, which most certainly was not the first such prolonged sanctioned atrocity in human history in the name of God? How many peoples have been waged war on, subjugated, even decimated, for holding other beliefs?

Christianity, which is the world's leading religion, is supposedly the most passionate and enlightened faith. Yet it has waged more religious wars and its exponents forced more cultures and races into conversion (while obliterating small groups that resisted such) than any other faith. In fact, it probably owes its top ranking more to conquest and intimidation than to the wisdom and convincing power of the tenets in the Bible and the teachings of Jesus and the apostles.

Islam, now the second largest religion, also spread its influence and gained followers with lightning speed so soon after its birth due to war and conquest. Even in the present, "jihad" or "holy war" is still being waged by a number of Muslim groups against "infidels." The Twin Towers horror was only one of many that "crusading" Muslim extremists have wrought upon the planet.

Adolf Hitler murdered 6 million Jews simply because they were Jews and supposedly all guilty, collectively and individually, of a plethora of crimes against non-Jews, including, of course, the murder of Jesus Christ – which had been the original cause of persecution of Jews in Christianized regions since most of them were driven out of Judea and forced to wander in many different lands.

The persistent and recurring purges and massacres of Jews in many European countries through the centuries - since the earliest days of the spread of Christianity as a religion accepted and even practiced by emperors and kings, in other words by officialdom in the first millennium of the Christian

Era - can be attributed to the only instance of deicide (killing of a god) that is directly imputed to an existing group of people.

It was very easy, and even logical, for Christians to hate the Jews on the grounds that they caused Jesus to be crucified. But this is the emotional, even shortsighted viewpoint. For it does not take into consideration that Jesus' apostles and original followers were also Jews.

Most important of all, Jesus was himself a Jew, who, if the Gospel accounts are to be believed, preached as a Jew, prayed to the Jewish God and died as a Jew. In fact, the cross on which he died had a sign that read "Jesus of Nazareth, King of the Jews".

Instead of regarding the strife that motivated some Jews to condemn Jesus as a racial or religious conflict, the entire matter must be considered simply as an internal quarrel between Jews of different persuasions.

To blame and hate all Jews for the crucifixion of Jesus will be equivalent to condemning and ostracizing all Americans for the assassination of Abraham Lincoln or John Kennedy.

Such is the myopic, often blind, adoption of sectarian attitudes by many followers of various religions that so many violent conflicts between different faiths have been wrought on peoples throughout history and some continue to fester up to the present.

The conflict between the Arab nations and Israel may have become religion-driven but it did not start out as such. Its root cause is the quarrel over land and territory. The Jewish refugees from Europe established the state of Israel on what they regarded as their people's ancestral homeland, which had been known as Palestine and occupied for many centuries by Arabs who were mostly Muslim.

In the wars that erupted as a result of the territorial dispute many of the other Arab states took the side of the Palestinians and the continuing conflict became a Muslim-versus-Jew affair.

The fact that the Middle East is the birthplace of their respective religions, with many sites considered holy by their followers situated within the areas being contested, has exacerbated the religious character of the hostilities.

Yet, the true differences of the Islamic and Jewish religions are not very sharp. Islam sprang from the ancient beliefs and traditions of the Bible, specifically what Christians call the Old Testament.

Thus, Muslim Arabs and Jews share legendary or religious ancestry going back to the patriarch Abraham; which is very plausible, for their peoples all belong to the Semitic family, having evolved from the same stock in the same region, with similarities in language and religion-related customs like circumcision and abhorrence of pork.

Too, neither side is denigrating the other's faith. In fact, many Muslims hold a special regard and affinity with followers of Judaism and Christianity, whom they call "people of the Book" (meaning the Bible) like themselves.

Still, things have spiraled so that most Muslims, including those outside the Middle East, consider themselves morally at war with Israel, even if some Arab nations, like Egypt and Saudi Arabia, have assumed a more tolerant stance towards the Jewish state.

Had there been no difference in religion in the first place, if the people that were settled on erstwhile Palestinian land were Muslims like the Palestinians it would be simply brothers in faith giving sanctuary one to the other. This is illustrated by the way Jordan, Syria and Lebanon have for decades now tolerated, even if grudgingly, the many Palestinian refugees in their territories.

Then again, if those people that established the state of Israel had not been Jewish, they would not have had to go there at all. They would not be the "chosen" pariahs and victims of Hitler and other religious bigots.

Another, perhaps more blatant, case of violent conflict fueled by difference in religion is that between Hindu India and Muslim Pakistan.

These Hindus and Muslims are literally brothers, for relatives are on both sides of their border and they all descended from natives of the Indian subcontinent. Originally part of what was known as British India, Pakistan was granted independence by Great Britain as a separate state to be the home of the Muslim minority in their erstwhile colony. Thus Pakistan and India became separate sovereign states despite being once one territory that was home to Hindu and Muslim as well as other religious minorities that coexisted in a certain degree of harmony and tolerance.

The partition resulted in divergent attitudes and interests, including struggle for control of the Kashmir region. Warfare has periodically broken out and, even when there is no officially-declared war or organized military operation, terrorist attacks have been perpetrated on both territories.

In the ongoing hostility between Hindu India and Muslim Pakistan, the hatred is so deep that one could no longer imagine that Pakistan was once part of India and that members of families and clans are scattered across the two nations even though some now belong to different faiths.

Obviously, had there been no difference in religion there would have been no partition into two states and no religious or national strife.

Here, we must also consider the bitter animosity between and among brothers in Islam - the Shiites and Sunnis. The ferocity and violence of this enmity must be compared to the hatred and cruelty between some Christians of different sects or differing views of their common religion – like the Protestants and Catholics in Ireland and the Inquisition against dissenters and innovators with the blessings of the Catholic hierarchy.

It is all too apparent that the existence of religious differences is at the root of so much violent, bloody hostilities. There is no logical way this situation can be changed; each religion is naturally fighting tooth and nail for survival, and some are even actively trying to expand their areas of influence and gain more and more followers, often through conversion – which puts them in direct competition for the minds, and tithes, of potential converts.

Since it is probably impossible to have only one religion to avoid conflict, couldn't mankind do without religion altogether?

Does humanity need religion?

Let us go back to John Lennon's "Imagine" and look at the entire first two stanzas:

"Imagine there's no heaven
It's easy if you try
No hell below us
Above us, only sky…

"Imagine all the people living for today…

"Imagine there's no countries
It isn't hard to do
Nothing to kill or die for
And no religion, too…

"Imagine all the people living life in peace."

Clearly, Lennon, dubbed "the intellectual Beatle", was pointing to religion as one of the greatest causes for war and the killing of people, equal, at the very least, to the existence of separate countries.

The song was, and still is, so universally popular that it is very doubtful all its fans fully understood Lennon's message, for it is unimaginable that there are that many atheists worldwide.

But religion is not without its virtues and has brought about some of the greatest blessings (pun unintended) for mankind and civilization. From man's earliest beginnings, the belief in the supernatural was instrumental in bringing about order and discipline that were essential to the survival and progress of clans, tribes and ever-growing communities.

All kingdoms and nations that rose to power and cultural and technological prominence in the ancient world consisted of people held together by a certain religion, either fanatically adhered to by them or forced upon them, or both.

It would be impossible to manage large groups of human beings without the binding strength, or coercive force, of a body of supernatural beliefs that will transcend the limits of physical threats and intimidation wielded by armed components of the leadership.

The need for a more powerful, yet less physically demanding, means of controlling people gave rise to the close relationship and cooperation between tribal chiefs and witch doctors, kings and high priests, and even led to the combining of the two forces – corporal and spiritual – in god-kings like the pharaohs of Egypt and the emperors of Rome and Japan.

That is also why Spain and Portugal, in their colonization of lands across the globe, employed both the sword and the cross to subdue the various peoples in places their colonizing forces found worth claiming. The inclusion of converting colonized peoples to the Catholic faith among their goals and modus operandi also gained for the Iberian global plunder – including the capture and trade of Africans for slavery - the imprimatur of the Roman Catholic Church.

It was under the guiding influence, oftentimes even coercion, of the Roman Catholic Church that the European kingdoms and countries managed to coexist for nearly a thousand years in relative peace among themselves.

Islam's spread across the Middle East, Africa, Europe and Asia, although facilitated by armed conquest, also brought peace among erstwhile warring tribes and kingdoms and imposed similar morals and values among peoples who used to have contrasting cultures and ways of life. Of course, there have been some abuses in the name of Allah in some societies at various points in time, but that has been done by practically all faiths throughout mankind's history.

There are and have been, to be sure, many instances when religion, in the process of maintaining peace and stability within a society, brought about intellectual stagnation and backwardness among the faith's followers. The main reason for this is the subordination of the believers' minds to the supposed infallibility and timelessness of the particular religion's teachings and doctrines, principles which were intended to prevent chaos and conflict, such as we have seen in more liberal environments.

This was what happened to Christians in the Medieval Ages. The strict adherence to the dogmas and policies of the Roman Catholic Church, which practically shut the door on new and dangerous ideas, with the collusion of kings and princes, whose interests lay in the maintenance of status quo, made most people no better than farm animals, content to find grain and forage to sustain them from day to day until they somehow eventually died.

Only the Renaissance, which saw the changing of attitudes and modes of thinking in so many fields – arts, politics, science, religion - saved the Christian world from stagnation in ignorance, bigotry, religious tyranny and institutionalized hopelessness for the common populace.

The state of most Islamic countries until recently appears to be the reverse of what took place in the Christian world. Islam was a more liberal and tolerant faith during the Medieval Ages, when Muslim caliphs allowed Christians and Jews religious freedom within their boundaries. Intellectual, scientific and cultural development flowered among the Muslims, while the Christians, as stated earlier, were mostly held in bondage to ignorance, bigotry and religious intolerance as symbolized by the Inquisition.

Military defeats leading to colonization by European powers of Muslim regions have somehow brought about radical changes to the principles and practices of Islam, causing many, if not most, Muslim societies to be run like monasteries. Historians have wondered how and why Muslim nations and societies suddenly lost their intellectual and technological capabilities such that they now lag behind most industrialized, mainly Christian, countries.

Perhaps the bitterness of military humiliation in the past caused them to retreat within themselves and somehow they found security and stability in closed and strict, albeit stifling, Islamic law and practices as preached and instituted by their religious leaders.

Some Islamic societies even enforce stringent censorship of most, if not all, television and radio programs - the two media that disseminate information and knowledge most quickly and with the greatest reach - to shield their constituents from potentially corrupting ideas and influences from the non-Islamic world. Women are made to follow strict modes of conduct as well as dressing regulations, to protect morals and prevent them from imitating the almost undressed style of attire in modern cultures.

The Arab Awakening that unexpectedly came about at the beginning of the year 2011 may, hopefully, bring about a new culture and environment of freedom and openness in some, possibly most, if not all, such Islamic nations.

Of course, even to this day, half a millennium after the Renaissance, the Catholic Church as well as some Protestant and independent sects retain policies and regulations that restrict their members' actions and thinking. The use of artificial means of contraception is still anathema among those Catholics who scrupulously follow the edicts of the Church. Jehovah's Witnesses and some minor sects forbid blood transfusion and organ transplants, even when members' lives are at stake, citing Biblical precepts.

One may wonder: in this age of super-science, super-technology and liberalism in most of the civilized world, hasn't religion become obsolete or, worse, become a hindrance to full-scale progress of individuals' minds and social norms and practices – indeed, to the march of civilization and human development?

Surely, the secular leaders of nations of today no longer need the threat of eternal damnation and the fires of hell to maintain order over their populations? Except, of course, in some Islamic countries and other, mostly small, nations, where cultures and the leadership structure, as well as the people themselves, are not prepared to function and manage without the steadying influence and discipline of religion.

Other than those isolated cases, it would seem quite likely that ultra-modern societies like the United States of America, the United Kingdom, Germany, etc., can rid themselves of their religious institutions without suffering dire consequences like a breakdown in civil order and an outbreak of all sorts of crimes.

That may seem possible, even probable, at first blush, but the significance of faith and the need for it, though seemingly unnecessary from the macro viewpoint, are very vital, and indispensable, to the individual faithful. And there are masses of faithful who cannot do without some religion or other even in the most advanced societies.

Since primitive man first felt the need for answers to the mysteries of the world around him, since he first encountered dangers and obstacles he cannot overcome but which his developing intellect cannot accept without being hopelessly overwhelmed by fear of the unknown, since he first became aware of his own and his kind's mortality which they cannot escape from - homo sapiens had needed a god, sometimes many gods.

The belief in gods and supernatural beings was the instant and all-encompassing solution to the mysteries and fears that besieged men's minds, that would otherwise have made life unbearable, filled with confusion and constant uncertainty and anxiety. Gods were the reason the sun appears at dawn in one horizon and then disappears on the other at dusk, taking away the light and bringing on the dangers that accompany darkness. Gods made the terrible lightning and frightening thunder, the violent storms and earthquakes, when they are displeased or angry.

The world, therefore, was not so strange and confusing, after all. And the best part was, man developed the belief that he can get into the good graces of those gods, thus avoiding the tragic consequences of their wrath, and, yes, possibly even getting rewarded with special blessings.

Among those rewards, naturally, was the banishment of man's greatest fear – death. Because they knew of no one who had lived on and on and could be called immortal, early humans became aware that everyone, sometime, somehow, dies. Now, if the gods could allow a human being continued life even after one died, then death lost much of its fearsomeness. Indeed, death was no longer final, nor a real end to existence. Mortals can become immortal.

In fact, such beliefs had grown so powerful in some cultures that suicide, when done for a perceived righteous cause, is done unhesitatingly, even joyfully; for a better, more glorious life is the reward for the sacrifice of one's earthly existence. Muslim suicide bombers and Buddhists who set themselves afire are some examples.

Voltaire said: "If God did not exist, it would be necessary to invent him." Indeed, humankind in all parts of the world, of all races, shapes and colors, invented varying versions of gods and supernatural beings. The need for a god or even many gods was universal but since there were different cultures and circumstances all around the globe, so were the gods or supernatural beings they invented quite different from one another.

Certain peoples worshipped the sun, mountains, lightning and thunder, even trees and animals. Others worshipped gods that were actually superhumans, often with human tempers, desires and frailties. Some worshiped unseen, indescribable gods with limitless powers.

In whatever form or substance, or lack of it, gods filled the need of humans, the most intelligent species, for comfort and assurance which their already incredible intelligence could not provide; a need which, most probably and logically, that very intelligence created. For intelligent homo sapiens is the only species we know that is conscious of his mortality and fully cognizant of his own inadequacies against the dangers, problems, struggles and travails that are part of life and existence in the natural world, as well as the world he has created through civilization and technological innovations all around him and throughout the globe.

The dog does not worry or fear nor is he even aware that he will die one day, by some way or another; at least, not as far as we know. Cattle do not realize that the foot-and-mouth disease spreading in nearby farms pose a direct danger to them. Birds do not think about the possibility of a forest fire wiping out their habitat; when it comes they just fly away and try to adapt some place else as best they can. Fish do not worry about being caught next season by trawling ships even if that is a perennial danger; they are fully occupied as it were trying to survive the day.

So man, the most supreme creature of the planet, with the most developed brain that allowed him to change the face of the earth, is the one most beset by terror about things to come, whether in the near or in the far future. He is the one who needs an intellectual and emotional crutch. That is true of every human being, whether Caucasian, Malay, Negroid, aborigine, or any other ethnicity.

So all humans in all corners of the world created some sort of god or groups of gods to be their crutch. With various forms of religious faith, humans could manage to face the uncertainties of daily existence, as well as the certainty of his death, with a considerable amount of courage and confidence. It is mostly the belief in a supernatural being and a life in the hereafter that helps people with terminal diseases live out their last days with equanimity, sometimes even grace and dignity, instead of going crazy at the thought of the approaching end.

A great many individuals, perhaps the overwhelming majority, then as now, observed the laws and accepted norms of behavior in civilized society, not because of innate goodness, but because of fear of punishment or disfavor from a deity.

Too, it is the belief that some heavenly aid will eventually relieve their sufferings and ordeals, end their miseries and give them a better, perhaps richer, life that allow many, perhaps most, people at the lowest strata of the economic pyramid to trudge on from day to day, enduring the present tribulations and persevering against all odds. If they did not have that belief, which gives them eternal hope, as well, of course, the fear of heavenly chastisement, then they would probably kill their employers and empty their cash drawers and safes, or band together to raid banks, supermarkets, all establishments that have things they want or need but could hardly get their hands on.

That need for an intellectual and emotional crutch still remains in the human psyche, despite all the advances in human knowledge and sciences. Despite, too, the harsh reality that many, perhaps the overwhelming majority, of their prayers do not get answered. They are just given by their religious advisers, or they concoct for themselves, various reasons why the divine power does not grant their wishes - reasons they happily accept rather than consider the possibility that prayer has no effect or power, or, the utterly unthinkable; that there really is no one to hear, much less grant, their prayers.

The need to keep the faith, the belief in a creator and savior, is so overpowering, so essential to the sense of well-being and even mere being of the faithful that they refuse to acknowledge the proof of evolution of life and living organisms - despite all those dinosaur and trilobite fossils – because evolution demolishes not only the sacred texts but also the principle of a grand design by an omnipotent and omniscient deity.

True, there may be some agnostics and atheists, but they comprise a very small segment of the entire population.

Further, most people with religious faith look down with disdain, sometimes even hatred, at agnostics and atheists and it is not easy to be among the nonbelievers. The faithful can accept people of other faiths more than they can those without any faith at all.

The fact that others, albeit of different faith, somehow believe in the existence of supernatural or divine power bolsters each believer's conviction that God exists, that mankind and the universe are part of a creation, of a kingdom ruled by a supreme and beneficent intelligence.

That there are those that do not believe in a god, the very foundation of man's existence in the minds of the faithful – which is to say, their very own existence – without being struck down by lightning from a wrathful heaven, is most unsettling. It shakes up the pillars of their view and creed, threatening to destroy the whole structure of each believer's reality.

If there were no gods, the faithful are no longer part of an exclusive circle of salvation, no longer special children of a divine benefactor or savior. That is entirely unacceptable, and unimaginable. It casts them into pure insignificance, virtual nothingness, with eternal life entirely out of the equation.

So they either try to convert the agnostics and atheists into their faith or at least to the belief in the existence of god, or ridicule them and look at them as evil and followers of the devil and consider them to be damned and doomed.

In many instances, those who doubt or do not believe in a deity have to keep their belief, or lack thereof, to themselves, or between them and others of similar suasion to avoid the negative reactions and attitudes of those with faith. It takes courage for an atheist to proclaim his mind among those who have religion.

Believers do not know the even greater degree of courage agnostics and, more specially, atheists had to muster to accept their own form of enlightenment – which is that the existence of a god either could not be proven or disproven, or is actually disproven by the logical and completely rational evaluation of things as they see them. In accepting the reality of a godless world, they had to forego the ideas of their own personal immortality and divine intervention and succor, which give comfort and hope and cheer to the faithful.

Nonbelievers pay a heavy emotional and mental price for their own form of belief. But it is a price their reliance on logic and intelligence must pay. There may even be among them some who would want to turn around, embrace some faith and enjoy the sense of security and well-being, as well as immortality, most faiths bring; if only they could sincerely believe like the faithful and disregard what their own hopelessly logical minds tell them.

If these nonbelievers would somehow become a majority in a society, then that society could do without religion and a truly purely intellectual and logical milieu will come about. That is most improbable, or it is not probable in the near and foreseeable future. But it is not entirely impossible, given enough time. For there surely are more atheists now than in the past, as more people have the intellectual freedom to reason out and discuss their thoughts without superstitious hindrances and physical threats like being burned at the stake by Inquisitors.

For the time being, and perhaps through the next century or so, many humans need religion. But ways must be found to prevent religious differences from resulting in armed conflict and social discrimination and bigotry. Otherwise, man, despite his supposed maturity as a social creature, will not find peace and goodwill. Valuable resources and much effort will have to be devoted to fighting or resolving religious discord, efforts and resources which could have been channeled to the betterment of the global human condition.

Yes, religion must be controlled and the various faiths must actively and sincerely find a way to coexist. They must find a way to tolerate one another, perhaps look at the ways they are similar, not the ways they are different.

OVERPOPULATION: FAILURE OF SUCCESS

We say that a species is successful if its population thrives and multiplies. But a species that is too successful will eventually bring about its own demise, or at least trigger a decrease in its population to pre-success levels, or to a point where it does not endanger itself.

When deer, for example, multiply as a result of the absence or paucity of its predators and natural enemies, they eventually deplete their food resources and grow thin and weak and die out of undernourishment or disease. Or certain predators eventually move in to take advantage of the great number of prey and in time cut them down to a ratio equaling the consumption rate of the predators.

Overabundance of predators depletes the prey and the predators eventually decimate each other in the fierce competition for food or starve due to excessive demands on prey species which have been diminished or have even totally disappeared.

Humans appear to have reached beyond the plateau of their optimum population and should have, like the other species, been drastically diminished by some natural phenomenon or another.

Human intelligence and technological advances - particularly in the last two centuries which also saw the greatest increase in human population - have, however, prevented man's succumbing to the laws of nature. He has abused nature's bounty but always found substitutes or ways to fill the gap, often by abusing other natural resources – by some or other device and method, he has kept on surviving, and thriving.

Through science and medicine, he has conquered most of the natural calamities and diseases that should have killed off many of his kind. Man also improved the systems of production of his food and other necessities, such that many, if not all, people, get what they need without having to struggle too much.

In bringing about his species' betterment, he has also brought about the extinction of many other species, both animals and plants. He has driven them off their natural niches in the ecosystem, destroyed habitats, even directly decimated such creatures that he consumed for food and other needs or that competed with him.

Everyone knows that we have been causing so much damage to the environment, not only through over-consumption and over-utilization of resources, but direct abuse of the planet's pristine state through pollution of the air, waters and soil, and destruction of forests, landscapes and rivers in our relentless pursuit of progress for industries and expansion of our communities.

So many studies have shown that many species in the seas have been overfished, many kinds of plants and animals have been made extinct or are in danger of extinction, the areas covered by forests have shrunk and are continuously dwindling.

Many groups and prominent world personalities have been devoting time, money, careers and lives in advocacies to save the planet. Governments have instituted laws and regulations to either curb destructive practices or minimize their effects.

But we really cannot stop most of our activities that are harming the environment. We could not however much we wanted to.

Because there are too many of us. There are so many people to be fed, clothed and housed. More and more cities and towns are growing and need more electric power, water supplies, transport systems. Even without the profit motive that drives industrial and manufacturing concerns to provide these needs, they still have to be filled, by governments if not anyone else, if the latter are to perform their unshirkable responsibilities to their citizens.

Besides the large-scale and organized destruction, there is also the piecemeal, but nevertheless widespread, clearing of forests and grasslands for crops and grazing and other individual needs of marginalized and destitute people in hinterlands, the indiscriminate hunting of wild animals for meat, fishing of already diminishing species in overcrowded fishing communities.

But how can we stop these people in Africa, Asia and South America from doing the only things that can sustain them, meager as they are, in their hand-to-mouth existence?

In these places, protecting and preserving the environment and the natural habitats of other creatures and those creatures themselves is like proclaiming a death sentence on whole communities and ethnic groups.

Clearly, controlling and, if possible, reducing the world's population is of the utmost importance to save both people as well as other living creatures and the planet itself.

Yet, there are big, indeed, gigantic institutions that are actually not happy about controlling the population in the first place.

Big business does not want the population to decrease. People running those financial, commercial and industrial octopi know it is in their best interests for people to keep increasing in numbers. More people means more patrons for their products and services. More people means more potential workers – more workers in the job market mean cheaper labor and, of course, greater profits.

Religion, ah, yes, that old scourge of human progress, also wants more people. More people mean more followers and donors to church coffers.

Even if many of those people being born should belong to other faiths, they are still potential converts to their fold. That is why, despite all the portents of doom arising from the world's overpopulation, Catholic popes, one after another, oppose artificial birth control, insisting on natural, fail-prone methods.

With such institutions against the controlling of population growth, when and how can we keep down our numbers so that we can ease the pressure on all sorts of resources and the environment?

We had been too successful in propagating our species, too successful for our own good and, alas, the good of the rest of the world – nay, the entire planet.

But we should not lose hope. We do not have the right to.

HUMAN EVOLUTION
IN REVERSION

With man's success in providing for his basic needs and protecting his kind from many of the dangers of existence in a world that is coming more and more under his control, he became a more compassionate creature. He felt the urge, even duty, to come to the aid of the poor, the infirm, the stricken - almost any of his fellowmen who had need for succor.

He became compelled to save, heal and nurture the sick, the elderly, the mentally deficient and the physically deformed and handicapped – and evolved as the most magnanimous creature on the planet.

Thus man has been doing, not only on a personal scope where the unfit person is a family member, but on an institutionalized mode, with certain agencies often specifically established for the task of looking after the helpless or less fortunate members of society.

Yet, that compassion for his fellow human beings has also brought about some of his more insidious problems. The caring for the diseased sometimes causes the spread of diseases among the healthy members of the community; sometimes the diseases become even deadlier as they mutate during the course of being subjected to drugs and therefore could not be cured by existing medical products and treatments.

Too, the preservation of the sick, the deformed and the handicapped, besides being a burden for the rest of the community, add to the numbers of the population. In most instances, the diseased, deficient and deformed even produce offspring, sometimes among themselves and sometimes in partnership with healthy members of the community.

Not only do the diseased, physically deformed or handicapped reproduce their kind, they sometimes even increase in numbers, adding to the burden as well as danger to the society that nurtures them.

Further, the preservation of these people has somehow adversely affected human evolution. Observe how other species, say elephants or geese or dogs, that grow into adulthood are very nearly equal to other members of their species in size, strength, intelligence and overall physical condition. This is because the weak and defective offspring, as well as the sick and aging among them, are quickly eliminated by the forces of nature which take their course unimpeded in the universal struggle for survival of the fittest.

The situation in human societies is in stark contrast to that. We see quadriplegics being looked after by robust caregivers, who could very well be devoting their efforts to more beneficial tasks for the greater good of society. There are also morons and common nitwits all around the very few intellectuals. The gap between the best and the worst specimens of homo sapiens is so vast yet they exist side by side in cities and towns. Such discrepancies in the physical and intellectual conditions of members of the same species could not have arisen in the natural world.

Further aggravating the already precipitous imbalance between intellectuals and mentally inferior individuals in most human societies is the fact that intellectuals, being mostly preoccupied with their professions and intellectual pursuits, produce few, if at all, offspring, depriving succeeding generations of their valuable genes. Meanwhile, the less intelligent individuals are multiplying like rabbits in many regions, particularly the underdeveloped countries.

In the same vein and on a macro scale, people of developed and prosperous nations are decreasing in number as well as in proportion to the populations of the poor countries.

This was the situation that once led Lee Kuan Yew of Singapore, when he was prime minister of the rich city-island-nation, to offer material and other incentives for intellectuals and professionals who would produce children.

Of course, we could not advocate the abandonment of the less fortunate and defective specimens of our species to their own unattended fate. It will be callous and tantamount to condemning them to certain death with, most probably, considerable prior physical suffering.

We could avoid doing that whilst still preventing most, if not all, of the ill effects their preservation in society brings about.

We have already accepted the quarantine or isolation of those with contagious diseases as necessary to protect the health of the rest of the population. We may further consider the sterilization of those with genetic defects or hereditary diseases so that we can prevent the birth of more of their unfortunate kind.

It may seem like a violation of their human rights but it will be a small price to pay for the higher purpose of putting an end to, or at least minimizing, the further emergence of weak, sickly and handicapped offspring. Then, too, it is also a noble cause to uplift and continually improve the human species – although not in the style of Hitler and his experiments at producing the perfect Aryan race.

There may appear to be obstacles to the business of sterilizing certain sectors of the community, including the reaction and possible refusal of those to be placed under such a program. But there are also obvious benefits that sterilization will bring to them.

For instance, a sterilized couple can enjoy sex without the burden of raising children, which will also give them more financial and physical freedom and time to engage in other pleasurable activities. They will be rid of the many worries and problems inherent in the upkeep of families and providing for the future of children.

If there are sterilized individuals who have a strong urge to care for young, particularly women with fervent maternal instincts, then they could, if they are able and qualified, be given the chance to care for the children of those women who are engaged in professions and other work and find raising offspring an added burden and hindrance to their careers. The sterilized "mothers" could even be in charge of day-care centers or orphanages.

It is also possible that as sterilization is accepted as a method to purify humankind, certain standards may be determined as prerequisites for procreation. Or as the field of genetic engineering advances in the foreseeable future, prospective parents may be able to choose the qualities and characteristics of their offspring and disable undesirable or defective genes.

It may seem like some kind of Brave New World and sound morally abhorrent now to certain individuals and groups, particularly the religious and so-called protectors of human rights and morality, but future developments and necessities may make these things more acceptable, even unavoidable.

In fact, the time may come when it will be immoral not to implement such practices for the good of mankind. If man is to enjoy life within a society, a planned and regulated population, with the physical, psychological, intellectual and other traits of individuals also regulated for optimum benefit of the community, is the most logical course.

The improvement of homo sapiens as an entire species will also contribute to bringing about the equality and harmony that will be the greatest pillars of Utopia. For as men and women all over the planet become more nearly equal in intelligence and health, their capabilities to do work, and naturally to make money, will also become more level.

But what, one may ask, about the necessity for inequality and poverty that has been the bedrock of civilization since the dawn of time? If men and women were more or less equal in capability and capacity to earn income, who would agree to do the lowly tasks? Who would handle the garbage and sweep the streets?

Worry not, we will find solutions for these problems. For that, after all, is what this book is all about.

DIFFERENCES BETWEEN INDIVIDUALS, RACES AND CULTURES: CONFLICT AND CONFUSION

Science, as well as religion, tells us that we – all us human beings, black, white, brown, yellow, green or whatever - must have had a common ancestor. That is only logical. It is highly improbable that a mouse here gave birth to a human baby and a chicken there hatched another human from her egg.

In the course of millions of years of evolution, homo sapiens has become a very diverse species. Such are the differences between human races that a horse, a donkey and a zebra, though belonging to separate species, appear more related than an Eskimo and an Arab, or a Bush pygmy and a Chinese.

The variations in physical size, skin and hair color, and other physical features were naturally results of the geographical and climatic conditions where each type of human developed. But there are some things unique among humans as compared to animals that evolved in different regions of the world.

<u>Language.</u>

A Great Dane will bark and the Pomeranian will know exactly what the big dog means and react in fear or reply with its own bark, albeit in a smaller, higher-pitched voice.

An Indonesian rooster will crow and make feeding sounds to attract Canadian hens and they will understand him perfectly.

But let a Japanese talk in Nihongo and a Nigerian will just scratch his head, or punch him in the nose if the tone of the Japanese sounds aggressive or insulting to him. Even Indians and Chinese, who share a long common national border, do not have the slightest inkling of what each other are saying in their respective native tongues.

In fact, many Chinese speak different dialects and languages and could not communicate even with their own compatriots. That necessitated the development of the Chinese form of writing in characters which are mostly symbols that can be understood by most of them, even if the symbols sound differently when read and spoken in the diverse languages of the Chinese peoples.

Some may think that differences in language may only be a hitch in communication but language barriers often also represent attitudinal gaps. Very often, the greater the differences in language, the greater also are the distances between regions where they are spoken and, thus, in geographical, climatic and cultural environments.

People from the same culture, the very same immediate community, sometimes misunderstand each other's words, or the meanings and contexts in which they were spoken, and get into quarrels – even when they speak the exact same language. What more with people with very different native tongues and cultures? Even if one tried to learn the other's language he may not entirely comprehend all the nuances and idioms of that tongue, or the cultural backgrounds of certain words and phrases, and speak inaccurately or misunderstand what is spoken to him.

So differences in language, which evolved as various groups of humans learned to explore and conquer different parts of the planet and which is meant to be a bridge between minds and, indeed, express those minds, become an obstacle to true communication and understanding between peoples.

Culture

The longer a people or group of people have lived together in a region, the more established and deeply ingrained the culture they developed through many generations would be.

This is good for that particular group of people, for they would be thinking and acting the same way in most of their activities and there would be order and harmony among them. But that may set them apart from peoples beyond their borders and cause problems when they have to interact.

Misunderstandings have arisen when two groups do not have the same appreciation of certain things. Thus their values and attitudes clash. Sometimes a people may not even have a word for a certain emotion or situation, which rarely occurs in their culture, so they do not understand it, or when they encounter such, they would not react as other peoples would who fully comprehend it or comprehend it differently.

For instance, before the last two centuries when cultures and civilizations became more exposed and tolerant of one another, monogamous Christian Europeans had felt disgust, even contempt, at non-Christian societies, like the Arabs, Chinese and Japanese where polygamy, concubinage, even homosexual relations were the practice or tolerated.

Also, if a married Chinese man showed amorous interest in a European's daughter the European would feel very insulted and perhaps even afraid of the "evil" Oriental's lecherous intent to include her in his harem of wives and concubines.

On the other hand, chivalrous Europeans used to kiss the hands of ladies they meet socially. That would be a hideous assault of propriety among some Eastern societies where women's hands, as well as their feet and faces should not even be seen by males who are not family members.

At present, western men love to ogle pretty women and are not ashamed to be observed doing so, and the women take their attention as a compliment - but such acts would be taboo in many Muslim countries, specially the Arab ones.

In the same way, modern women love to dress sexily, often almost exposing their most feminine parts to tease men and catch their attention. They would be condemned in Islamic parts as well as certain areas in the West, like the Amish communities, where people of certain faiths believe women should be modest, even prudish.

Such contrasts in thinking have become wide-scale problems through history because they have caused certain groups to think of others as evil and dangerous to their own people's beliefs and way of life. They have been the seeds of racial hatred and suspicion, of refusal to accept one another as true equals. They have become obstacles to peace and compatibility and sparked wars and ages-old hostility.

Religion, like language, is a very vital part of culture - indeed, many cultures evolved from a religion. But even where religion is not a direct part or influence on the culture, the traditions and beliefs may be so deeply ingrained as to have the force of religion.

For instance, certain Oriental peoples put a high value on "saving face", meaning they want to avoid total humiliation even in situations where they are totally in the wrong or helpless. They must be allowed to make concessions or "give in" while getting some token concession in return. Otherwise, they will adamantly hold their ground even if it leads to dire consequences. Sometimes, "losing face" is deemed equivalent to dying or some similarly grave injury. If the side they are dealing with does not understand this, the results may be very costly and tragic, possibly for both sides - when something as simple as allowing the Oriental to surrender without giving up his sword could have ended the problem.

The white Americans offered to buy from the Indians the land which the former wanted to use for agriculture and other such purposes, but the Indians did not have a notion of land being property and being sold. Also, unlike the immigrants who came from lands an ocean away, the natives had an intrinsic attachment to their homelands. The whites on the other hand felt that the intransigence of the native Americans was just a manifestation of their being ignorant savages and an unreasonable hindrance to the whites' acquisition of the lands they needed for ranches and farms.

Such divergence and incongruence of cultures and thought processes resulted in the bloody and often brutal Indian wars.

* * *

Language and culture have been sources of national and racial pride through the ages, for they distinguish and give identity to peoples of different lands. But they are also barriers to international communication and understanding and have through those ages caused conflict and suffering.

We probably could not expunge all these throughout the planet and impose one universal language and one universal culture. Yet, there has been much progress in bridging the gaps and breaking down the barriers of languages and cultures as a natural and inevitable result of globalization and instant electronic communication and exchange of information, ideas as well as products through the internet.

In another half-century or so, perhaps we will no longer be lost in the Tower of Babel.

OTHER HUMAN DIFFERENCES

Besides economic circumstances, language and culture humans have other differences that cause discontent and unhappiness or conflict.

As earlier mentioned, humans are different in physical characteristics and attributes both between races and individuals. Not only is the Philippine Aeta so much different from the tall blond Caucasian; or the Japanese from the Masai, sometimes people from the very same stock can look so different they may as well have belonged to different races.

The modern and intelligent and "correct-thinking" person may feel or think that these physical differences no longer mean a thing.

But they have influenced the thinking and attitudes of countless generations before, and they still do.

The notion that white is good and black is bad caused white men to regard blacks and other colored peoples as evil, or at least inferior. Although Chinese and Japanese are also fair-skinned, the fact that they look different with their chinky eyes also made them a lesser type of human - the yellow race. Yellow, in the western mindset is the color of cowards.

It is not, of course, only the American or European who is guilty of racial bigotry. Each racial group has its own beliefs about their own superiority over other races. People everywhere also used to think that different physical looks made for different mental and behavioral characteristics. Thus racial hatred and distrust have long festered in the psyche of countless generations and civilizations.

Of course, there is also some truth to the belief that races have some traits peculiar to each or that they do not necessarily share with everybody else or that are more pronounced in some than others. The geographical separations that are part and parcel of the development of different races also spawned differences in ways of life, culture and language, as well as beliefs and attitudes. Coupled with physical differences, it is understandable why and how racial discords were magnified and perpetuated through the ages.

The racial profile of serial killers, including serial rapists, in the United States who are generally found to be white males between 20 to 40 years of age, or thereabouts, still has to be thoroughly studied by anthropologists, psychologists and sociologists. But there, indeed, seems to be a tendency for white people to be "mad" in both negative and positive ways.

Yes, there are white serial killers and serial rapists and rapist-killers, but the people who devote their lives selflessly in the pursuit of knowledge and the achievement of noble goals that do not bring material rewards – sometimes without even so much as recognition in return as the deeds are done in total anonymity - are also mostly white people.

White people went to the poles, climbed Mt. Everest, discovered the workings of the solar system and the galaxies. Mostly white people lead the thankless and often dangerous struggle to preserve the environment and protect endangered species.

Meanwhile, Asians, particularly Malays, are more prone to going berserk and attacking anybody and everybody in mindless rage - running amok is the popular term - whether substance-induced or otherwise. Those with Latin blood seem to be more quick-tempered than other people.

Despite such racially-related tendencies, however, most of the radical generalizations of the different races that have been the root of animosity and hostility in earlier times were greatly exaggerated and were often spawned by superstitions or isolated incidents that were unfairly broadcast as reflecting the character of an entire racial group.

In this period of enlightenment, many of the misconceptions have been cleared and the barriers they engendered have been broken down. But not entirely. There are still remnants of the racial and cultural animosities, some endangering the lives of individuals as well as entire communities – like the white against black conflict that still somehow remains in South Africa and in places and among individuals in the United States, the often violent conflicts between various tribal groups in Central Africa, Afghanistan and many other places.

Among individuals, even when belonging to the same racial group, the differences in physical characteristics range from being tall or short, thin or slim as against heavy or obese, then the most sensitive difference of all: beautiful versus ugly.

Until recently, before the onrush of technological development, greater size - height and mass – was considered desirable, at least for the human male. Greater size meant greater physical strength, which was very important for war or work.

However, in an age when few wars are fought, with some generations in some parts of the world never experiencing combat, and with weapons that kill the enemy and devastate his battlements with the simple act of pressing a button; where most work is done by machines that do not require much effort, least of all thick muscles, such that women can very well replace men in most tasks - physical size does not mean much. Only if one is playing basketball or American football or is a bodybuilder will height and bulk be of value.

Fact is, greater size should be considered a handicap or burden in majority of the aspects of present existence and function. Greater size naturally entails greater consumption – of food, clothing materials, even water and oxygen. It also requires more space. Already, some airlines had recently contemplated charging extra for overweight or extra large passengers. Even when using private transportation, very huge people would not easily fit into compact cars, or they would at least be uncomfortable during the trip. Astronauts have to be small, since additional weight will consume more fuel and the limited space in spaceships will hamper their movements.

We know, of course, that among primitive people – like in many animals – greater size and agility would have been premium traits. Thus, bigger men – and perhaps bigger women, too – would be considered "beautiful" and preferable as mates. Thus, we can see that in most instances, particularly amongst human groups within the same region, the more progressive groups are often of greater size, with the smaller ones usually marginalized.

The aspect of beauty is a very nebulous and subjective one. The accepted modern standard in most developed societies, influenced in no small degree by western culture and media, conforms to the current tastes of the west. Tall, slim women and equally tall and strongly-built (but not too muscular) men – well, that is the general norm. Certain individuals, of course, have their own peculiar preferences and tastes.

Some women feel older men – often old enough to be their fathers – are more attractive. Some men like fat women.

In some African cultures, the standards for female beauty range from large, deliberately and continually distended lips to necks made elongated by wearing an ever-increasing number of metal neck bands.

The Chinese, up to very recently, considered small, bound and deformed female feet as a prerequisite for sexual attractiveness and normally developed female feet were undesirable and associated only with the lower classes.

In contrast to the present western idea of slimness as the mark of female beauty, the norm several centuries ago – as can be gathered from classical nude paintings – was for fat or at least very fleshy women.

It would seem inappropriate to discuss beauty in the same breath as economic, racial and cultural differences, but the biases and insecurities that arise from prevailing standards in certain societies create another chasm, specially where various ethnic groups intermingle and a certain group's physical features are regarded as more desirable or superior, or another group's as disgusting or inferior – like in matters of skin color, stature and facial characteristics.

Certain establishments and organizations put a premium on certain physical traits for people they hire or accept as members. In a cosmopolitan world, physical differences should not count at all, except when absolutely unavoidable and as matters of necessity. But that is at present merely theoretical, merely an ideal that is hypocritically paid lip service to.

People, specially women, must realize that no trait is really more beautiful. Some dark-complexioned women want whiter skin. Many fair-skinned people spend good money to get tanned. Beauty, indeed, is in the eye of the beholder.

Some societies, particularly the American, have started to avoid negative or hitherto derogatory descriptions and classifications of people. That is a good first step toward demolishing biases and misconceptions of races and individuals.

In time, women will no longer have to spend so much time and money trying to look like somebody else. Men will not go to gyms to develop muscles that are not genetically inherent to them and just find easier ways to stay physically fit, which should be the most sexually appealing trait of all.

Dogs do not discriminate among themselves, it does not matter if one is a Chihuahua or a Great Dane. A French poodle does not even notice if the dog next to it is another, more handsome, French poodle or a fierce-looking American bulldog.

A Thoroughbred stallion will mate with a receptive draft horse. A Shetland pony will even romp and play with a donkey.

Animals do not have biases, they accept fellow creatures of the same or like species as they are. And, of course they do not try to be what they are not.

It may seem lowly animal behavior and instinct, but it is more social and, in the final analysis, more human.

URGE FOR ACQUISITION: BOON AND BANE

Throughout the history of mankind, the greatest driving force for his actions, besides the instinct for survival, has been the desire to acquire material things. In most instances, this desire has far outstripped the sexual urge – for while men and women at the peak of their sexual appetites have at least an equal appetite for acquisition, men already incapable of sex, either too obese or too old for the act, and even women who were not known to be at all libidinous, also show insatiable greed for wealth and even more wealth.

This urge or instinct, insofar as we know, could have evolved only as a consequence of the advent of civilization, as man began to live in larger, better organized communities and the best food no longer went to the best hunter, or the most desirable female to the strongest warrior, but to the one who had the most gold, or money, or whatever went for currency at that time and place.

This is very plausible as individuals in primitive tribal groups do not show as much acquisitiveness as more civilized people. Where people live in caves or sleep on tree branches there is a very short limit to the material objects he can keep. A man or a woman could not hunt or forage while lugging his or her earthly possessions which, presumably, could not be left behind in the tribal cave lest others covet and take them.

We do not know if primitive people did not develop the instinct for acquisition, or if the seed for that instinct already existed in their subconscious but remained dormant, because it was impossible to act it out; or if the urge grew out of improving intelligence and capability to hold on to possessions as a result of technological and organizational development.

Once man stepped out of the simple mode of existence when he had to chase or strike down his prey by himself or pick fruits and edible leaves from the forest on his own or with the help of his mate and offspring, we can presume that he began to want to acquire and retain things that are of immediate and/or long-term benefit to himself.

He may have wanted an extra spear or bow, more arrows in reserve, more women to gather food and tend to his crop. Then he may have wanted not just any horse to ride on the hunt or in traveling but a good one, possibly the best horse – better yet, several horses, several of the best horses available.

But the lust for acquisition must have been fueled to unlimited levels with the establishment of beads, gold, or whatever form of currency was accepted, for then he did not have to physically possess twenty horses and a corral to keep them, along with the problems of caring for them. He can have a piece of gold that has the value of twenty horses, which he could have anytime he needed them with the simple act of paying with his gold piece.

He can have several of those pieces of gold, and the power that such wealth naturally brings with them. All he needed was a pouch to put those pieces of gold in wherever he went, or if he had a house, he could keep them in a secret spot which no one could get to without being noticed by the man or his wives and children.

Eventually, people, as they became more established in cities and kingdoms, gained the capability to possess wealth equivalent to many times what they will need or be able to use in their lifetime, or even in their immediate descendants' lifetimes and, yet, most of those who got to possess such riches never stopped trying to acquire more and ever more.

It is thus evident that the urge to acquire property goes beyond the need to provide for the individual's needs and wants; it is an urge to acquire for the sake of acquiring. There is no saturation or satiation point, the richest man would not slow down despite his vast fortune. Bill Gates would no more retire to just enjoy his billions than he would deliberately stop breathing.

It is possible, even probable, that Bill Gates may no longer be consciously driven by a desire to acquire more wealth but by the sheer enjoyment of improving his computer softwares and programs and remaining the leader in his field - although achieving those things will most certainly and inevitably increase his already dizzyingly huge piggy bank. But if he were to be made aware of an impending possibility that he may lose a handful of billions, which would not really hurt him at all, he certainly would take steps to prevent its occurrence and if there were, instead, the opportunity to add to his fortune, he will most probably grab it.

Since the most primitive homo sapiens developed the urge to take or acquire more than his own most immediate needs – more fruit than he can eat until his hunger is relieved, meat for the next day or two instead of only as much as he can cram into his belly, or

food to take back to his mate and offspring that were waiting in some cave or secluded spot in the jungle – the seeds of competition, acquisitiveness and greed were born, and, along with them, human inequality and continuing and eternal conflicts.

There are a few exceptions to this sad state of human social existence – like among some American Indian tribes and very primitive peoples who maintain the idea and actual practice of communal ownership or sharing of all the bounties of nature and whatever benefits gained from their common, and sometimes even individual, efforts Such may be said, too, of the kibbutzim of Israel and some hippie and religious groups.

By and large, however, human beings and societies, and the world's nations, too, continually compete for a bigger share of the pie, sometimes taking, or trying to take, the entire pie. Through the course of millennia of human social and intellectual development, this has come to be regarded as the natural course of man's existence; in some instances and by some social classes and particular individuals, it is considered the ultimate and constant, unchanging objective of all human endeavor. Thus, the successful professional, already rich from the handsome rewards reaped from his field of expertise, will invest in the stock market or open a restaurant, instead of just enjoying the luxurious existence his accumulated funds entitle him to.

Many moneyed people even band together and pool their resources to gain advantage in the pursuit of profit and more wealth. Too, some groups organize cooperatives or corporations to help them cope with economic forces that more easily overwhelm individuals and small entities, forces which large, well-funded institutions can weather and even turn around to their advantage because of the flexibility afforded by their bigness and vast resources.

This philosophy drove the countries of Europe to form an organization that will enable them to compete or deal with wealthier giants, particularly the US and Japan, on a more or less equal footing. Thus was born the European Economic Community which morphed into the European Union.

The United States, Canada and Mexico formed the NAFTA, as some sort of reaction to EU, while the Asian nations have been working on the Asia-Pacific Economic Cooperation to find a way to strengthen themselves as the world evolves into a market and arena of macro-entities.

The ceaseless struggle for material gain and advantage has been the single biggest cause of human suffering, for individuals as well as social groups and entire nations, as there naturally would be winners and losers – with the winners usually exploiting their success, and the advantage gained from such success, to achieve greater and long-lasting, even almost unending dominance. Thus, we see many cases of the rich getting richer while the poor get ever poorer.

When a man or a woman gains wealth, he or she rarely proceeds to enjoy the full benefit and pleasure such wealth will afford – like the professional who invests in the stock market - but would use most, or even almost all, of the acquired wealth to acquire even more, either through direct investments or as leverage to facilitate further material gain, thus progressively expanding the gap between his or her circumstances and those of the less fortunate people in their community.

Let us not, however, make any mistakes about this insatiable urge of homo sapiens; it is not an entirely harmful one. Fact is, the desire for wealth, limitless desire for limitless wealth, has been the impetus for progress, particularly the industrial and technological aspects of it.

Large factories, with ever-improving machineries, would not have been possible without hugely wealthy people, in their desire to be even much richer, to put up the capital. We could not have seen the building of great ocean-going ships, or airliners, steel mills and pharmaceutical laboratories, as well as the putting up of scientific research grants and setting up of institutions for discovering and developing learning in various fields.

It may seem like the owners of the factories have been getting the bulk of the benefits from the deal but if we did not have General Motors, Mitsubishi and Bayer, we would not have workers driving cars and living in comfortable houses or apartments, while being kept healthy most of the time and having life expectancies more than double those of people who lived a couple of centuries ago.

Those workers would be trying to squeeze crops out of small farms and living in huts, and so will the owners of General Motors and other companies, of course. And they will all be plagued by many pains and diseases that we routinely cure with a regimen of pills today, as they approach their deaths which, before the advent of modern science and technology, usually came before the age of 40.

(General Motors is repeatedly referred to even though the industrial giant went bankrupt and was kept in operation only with the billions of dollars in assistance from the US government, because GM, prior to the economic meltdown of 2008, was THE ultimate symbol of industrial success in the world - the leader in income, in production of automotive products, in number of international subsidiaries and workers employed worldwide. No other company, as of this writing, comes close to the status it has attained in about half a century of corporate dominance.)

As poverty has been important for the progress of civilization, so has the other side of the coin – which is wealth or affluence, which could not come about if there did not exist the desire for material acquisition. This lust for riches, call it greed if you will, has its rightful and indispensable niche in the scheme of things.

Lest it be misunderstood, it is not only the rich and the successful who harbor that greed, that compelling desire for acquisition. The poor, even the very poor, also have such a desire burning within the deepest recesses of their souls; it is just that the rich are the ones who got to realize their wish and the poor are still hoping their time will come.

How can the poor be helped out of their condition? We cannot ignore them and leave them to their misfortune forever. Specially not in this day and age when despite poverty some of them become highly educated and could find ways to organize the teeming masses and put the world at a standstill simply by going on strike and refusing to work. Yes, they do not have to go up in arms and unleash violence to make people at the higher echelons listen, although they could also do that, with disastrous results for everyone.

Economic disparity begs to be corrected all over the world.

Suppose, to quickly solve the problem, we increased the compensation of the workers at the bottom of the pyramid. Easy enough, right? If the street sweeper and the farm hand are making out miserably on X dollars or X euros or X whatever, then let us double it to XX dollars or XX euros or XX whatever. If that is not enough to make them comfortable then make it XXX whatever.

Where will all that additional money come from? Remember that you will have to double or treble the income of those at the base of the economic pyramid, which is the largest sector in the community. The only possible source of that would be the income and/or wealth of those on the upper strata, and since they are progressively lesser in number, it will mean impoverishing them by a very considerable, possibly impossible, degree.

That is looking at it abstractly. To illustrate in a more practical manner, let us suppose a corporation with 10,000 workers wanted to improve the lot of everybody in the lower echelons, which is about 80 percent of the total personnel. It will have to be a corporation making so much money to be able to significantly increase the compensation of that large a number of people.

And what about the upper 20 percent? If the wages of the lower 80 percent are improved by a substantial amount, then they might overtake some of those in the upper 20 percent and this situation will again have to be corrected. Possibly the corporation's income will be used up in the payroll and benefits of the work force, such that the owners and stockholders will decide to place their investments elsewhere.

Granting that there are such companies with so much income, how many of them are there in the world? Surely they will be in the minority and the practice of giving even the lowliest of the work force enough compensation to give them comfortable living standards could not be a widespread one. So the problem of poverty or economic disparity will still be largely with us.

Then, too, there is the problem of human motivation.

If the poor who perform the dirty and backbreaking tasks are no longer poor, will they still do their work? It will be a stupid dockhand who will not save up on his considerable income so that in a few years he can set up some small business of his own and he can quit his tough job. What more of the skilled workers? The mechanics will strive to establish their own auto repair shops.

Oh, the garbage collectors will surely aspire to find a new, more respectable trade as soon as they can. As small entrepreneurs, perhaps. Or maybe they can save up for a college education and become professionals.

Factories will soon lose their work force. So will city halls as well as national governments.

Everything will stand still. Or retrogress. For it is not human nature to love doing hard and menial work. We are not ants, with each type performing its tasks without question or need for motivation.

The fact is: as things are now, and as they have been since humans became organized in a society – and as has been said earlier - poverty, in varying degrees, must exist hand in hand with affluence for civilization and society to function.

Even the most powerful army cannot exist without orderlies to attend to the needs of the officers, or bottom ranks to tend to mess duties, and so on. No Julius Caesar or Alexander the Great or George Patton could have charged to victory with every man acting as a general or even a captain or even as a plain warrior. In the same way, General Motors could not finish one automobile if everyone there was an engineer.

So it seems like we are caught in a vicious cycle. We want to help and protect the people at the bottom but we could not do without the moguls, who are providing the former jobs and livelihood, as natural components of their efforts to grab an ever larger share of the pie, the same pie the poor are trying to scrape more of.

What about curbing the greed, the lust for acquisition? Could we not tell the very rich to stop trying to get richer, be contented with what they already have?

But still that would not solve the problem. That would only freeze the situation at a status quo. The rich will be as rich as they are and the poor will remain in their miserable conditions, and worse because then they would have no hope of rising above the rubble.

Yet there is a way we can bridge the gap but it would require reorienting people and realigning their sense of values, not only figuratively but also literally. It will not be easy or painless but it is something the world will have to undergo, soon or late, but the sooner the better, if humanity is to achieve not only some sort of Utopia but the fulfillment of being truly and completely human in the highest sense of the word.

REVISING SOCIAL VALUES

The lust, or itch, for acquisition has grown out of proportion to a human's individual or even familial needs and could be considered, in extreme instances, to be of insane scope.

The poor want to be rich, and being rich is a relative idea and, apparently, an endless road. The rich want to be more than rich, they want to be millionaires, millionaires want to be multi-millionaires, multi-millionaires want to be billionaires. Billionaires don't rest to enjoy their wealth and always strive to get ever more.

When one is penniless, he imagines he will be happy if he gets a thousand bucks. When he gets the thousand, yes, he is happy – but only for a while. When he gets used to always having a thousand or two, he wants for more. Always, there is a lot more money, so much more wealth, to covet and aspire for.

Is happiness, true lasting happiness, attained somewhere in the process?

Is the man with a million dollars a million times happier than one who only has a dollar? Is the guy with one hundred million dollars a hundred times happier than the guy who only has a measly million?

Suppose a guy can afford to buy one Lamborghini and another can buy twenty Lamborghinis as well as twenty

Ferraris. So what? One can only drive and ride one car at a time, right? Or one person has one roast turkey for dinner while his neighbor can buy a thousand roast turkeys. What good are the nine hundred ninety-nine extra roast turkeys for?

Ten, twenty, thirty palatial mansions all over the world. How many houses can one live in? How many beds and rooms does one need to sleep? Sure, the more houses one has, the more prestige he has, but while people talk about the Rothschilds or the Gettys having that many villas, do the Rothschilds and Gettys really get to enjoy those villas? How long do they get to stay in each?

How many among the scores of rooms in each villa actually get to be used by either the owners or their guests, and, if at all, how often?

Socialites and movie stars normally appear in parties and social events wearing expensive designer clothes and dazzling jewels.

Does Madonna have to strangle her lovely neck with strings of pearls and diamonds to attract attention? Would Elizabeth Taylor have been less of a celebrity and superstar without a glittering tiara?

Would Princess Diana have been less loved and adored if she did not wear Chanel or Versace creations and just picked off some rags from a department store rack? Did Elvis Presley need to sport a 24-karat gold crown to be The King?

Does anybody care whether or not Franklin Delano Roosevelt or his chauffeur admired Renoir? Would history have been different if Winston Churchill liked French cuisine better than old English fare and preferred this or that French restaurant?

So many seemingly stupendous and important things are really quite meaningless or at least not that important or significant when viewed in the cold light of logic. The society pages of newspapers and gossip talk shows about the rich and famous focus on their profligate ways and mind-boggling displays of extreme affluence. How lavish their parties are, how fountains of champagne overflow while caviar and lobsters and other rich foods almost swamp the guests.

What good, really, are all those? All those stupid, wasteful acts and gestures that set them apart from lowly mortals who have to toil long hours just to keep body and soul together?

If we look long and hard at the overall picture, many of the world's wealthiest people exert a lot of serious effort to make so much money that they can thereafter throw away. It is, after all, the only way the rich can show their richness, by squandering money one way or the other. By confronting the poor with the vast gap in their stations in life or by showing the other rich folks that they can burn as much or more money.

In other words, just bragging rights. That is all that truly great wealth is really good for.

Is it worth it? Should a man toil, and cheat, and scheme so he can show his neighbor that he can spit farther? That he has a larger swimming pool? Or that he has several cars that guzzle fuel instead of sipping it, cars that could take him more quickly to his death with more devastating effects on his mangled corpse?

Is it so important that our wives could wear so many sparkling stones which they have to keep hidden most of the time in some bank vault? Or that we have a limousine that stretches the length of two cars and take up so much space on the road? That we imbibe one-hundred-fifty-year-old wines instead of last year's crop of grapes?

Then, if we are not among those successful and lucky enough to be in the exclusive club, we simply idolize them, envy them, try in various ways to emulate them.

Most people do not know that it is not a very happy exclusive club. That it is not ONE exclusive club. For among the rich and famous, there are hierarchies and strata, one who is rich and famous is not part of the club for the VERY rich and the VERY famous; the latter, of course, are not *in* in the special enclaves of the ULTRA rich and ULTRA famous. Mere millionaires are looked down upon by the multimillionaires who are naturally not in the league of billionaires.

Even those who belong in the same financial strata are not all equals. The old rich, either those with aristocratic blood or who belong to a long line of wealthy ancestors, disdain the nouveau riche, specially if the new rich made their fortunes from less than elegant enterprises - like a chain of laundry shops or funeral parlors, or if the fortune came about by accident, like a lottery, or inheritance from a distant relative, or discovery of oil in a fallow farmland. It isn't simply how big one's fortune is, it also matters how long one has had that fortune – and whence it came.

So if you think hitting the lotto jackpot or finding a gold mine under your house will get you to hobnob with Donald Trump and the Prince of Monaco, you are way off base. You will just get to be in the crowd of some shopkeeper who got to establish a chain of supermarkets, or the tragic Anna Nicole Smith, whose super knockers were able to excite an old billionaire to his quick end and got her to lay claim to a chunk of his hard-earned fortune (which, unfortunately, she really failed to get her hands on until her own mysterious death – although she made good money just the same in the entertainment industry, thanks to her awesome figure).

Of course, if you are a mafioso or a Colombian drug lord, no matter how many billion dollars you have stashed away or control for your organization, you will not be in the Buckingham Palace guest list, nor will you be dining at the Waldorf-Astoria. You most probably will be dining in different hideouts with only your confederates and bodyguards to keep you company.

As has been said earlier, being rich, like joining a corporate organization, is not reaching a plateau. It is still a pyramid. Lowly millionaires could not just get in the circles of their betters, the multi-millionaires. And the billionaires, well, they are a lonely lot – they are few and usually far from each other's company, and are often at war with each other in the struggle to control industries and even governments.

So being rich does not give one blanket bragging rights. There is almost always somebody else, or many others, the rich have to bow their heads to. There is no apex to reach and enjoy in being rich; one does not really get to be on top of the world. It is a big mountain and the peak is quite a long ways off, and reaching the top is not like conquering Mt. Everest.

Being among the super-rich does not give one a long-lasting high that one can fondly and proudly relive over and over again, but rather puts one in a very high pressure situation that one has to fight hard continually to keep and defend, for so many others covet one's wealth or at least some chunks of it and they will always be trying and pitching and scheming.

Such is the stratification of the rich people's club that there was once a multi-millionaire who, when told by his accountant that his fortune which once amounted to over 100 million dollars had shrunk to twenty million, committed suicide because he had become *poor*. Indeed, he has, not in the stark reality of the ordinary human being who must find a loaf of bread and a chunk of cheese to put into his belly – but by the standards of his bejeweled, limousine-riding peers.

One may posit that more than bragging rights, great wealth means great power, whether in politics, in society and/or in controlling and/or influencing the economic life of nations.

Yes, there is also that. But the powerful do not always win; they do not always have their way. For they also have enemies equally powerful, or even more so, or if none could match their power one-on-one then groups may form and pool group members' strengths to overwhelm them.

At any rate, there is hardly any peace or respite for the very, very rich and very, very powerful. It is an endless contest they are locked in. If they do not wish to compete, then they lose outright. The very rich cannot afford to rest on their laurels, or their money, for the world at large will not let them enjoy their riches in quiet solitude, for the world at large covets what they have.

Selling everything and keeping the money in banks to get away from the rat race may seem like a solution, but there are always thieves to steal their valuables, or if most are kept in bank vaults then there are kidnappers who will take their loved ones for huge ransom, or, if not those cheap hooligans, the government will be eating away the fortune through taxes, or the money will be losing value because of inflation. No, the very rich have to keep fighting to stay where they are.

So why would people want to be rich, even very rich?

Because there is that notion that having more, lots of everything, specially money, will make a person happy.

On the contrary, there are so many stories of immensely rich people who never became happy. Howard Hughes was the legendary symbol of the poor rich guy. Christina Onassis, sole heiress to storied billions, led a sad short life, dying at the ripe old age of 37.

Princess Diana, despite being the world's most glamorous and widely-adored personality, who may not have been personally super-wealthy but could probably have had anything she wanted just by asking for it, suffered terribly through her brief 36-year stay on the planet.

Her ex-husband Prince Charles, the most famous crown prince in recent history, has not been very happy either. He has had to endure many years of hiding his relationship with his true love, Camilla Parker-Bowles, who was married to another man; and even with Diana gone and Camilla divorced, they could not be with each other all the time or even most of the time as many people, most importantly Charles' mother Queen Elizabeth II, considered it improper for them to be seen together.

They only gained social acceptance when they married in 2005, after suffering years and years of scandal and embarrassment – which, to be sure, were a direct consequence of Charles' being Crown Prince, rather than a commoner who would have been free as a bird to live as he pleased with the light of his life.

To think that the world at first regarded it as a storybook romance, a fairytale love story - for Charles and Diana, the future king and his future queen.

Of course, we all know of the countless tragedies of movie stars and singers. Elvis Presley, in his time the most famous singer, adored by women and imitated by men all over the world, never knew true happiness until he died from drug overdoses at 42. Marilyn Monroe, once the ultimate sex symbol, died alone, at 36, with not one loving man beside her, though almost every red-blooded male desired her.

The latest super celebrity to pass away at a relatively young age, and almost still at the prime of his life and career, was Michael Jackson, King of Pop. Everyone knows Michael did not enjoy a glorious, blissful life in his Neverland fantasy haven. He had earned billions through his dizzying career but he was not, through the greater part of his life, truly happy.

Not only have fame and fortune at times failed to provide happiness for those who gained them; in quite a number of instances, fame and fortune, and power, actually caused the unhappiness and even tragic ends of their possessors.

How many political figures lost lives or suffered tribulations and dragged their loved ones along in the morass of troubles their possession of, or quest for, power brought them? From Julius Caesar to the Kennedy brothers to Yitzhak Rabin, great men were cut down by rivals or less worthy individuals.

Then, of course, there were those powerful people who so abused their lofty status and got lost in the intoxicating milieu of privilege that they were forcefully and humiliatingly brought down either by the people they dominated and mistreated or by rivals who capitalized on their abuses to justify their removal.

It is very clear that great wealth and great power do not translate into great happiness; more often than not, they bring about either great misery or great pressure and little reason, or time, to enjoy one's life in the truest sense.

Queen Elizabeth I, who had one of the longest reigns and was among the best loved monarchs of England, put it so succinctly when she said: "To be a king, and wear a crown, is a thing more glorious to them that see it than it's pleasant to them that bear it."

We all know that there have been many instances when the possession of wealth was the very reason the possessors came to grief. Take the sad ends met by two Johns. The first was country singer John Denver who crashed to his death while flying his private plane. The second was John F. Kennedy Jr., heir to a great name and great fortune, who also crashed in a private plane, along with his wife and sister-in-law. Had these two Johns not been so rich that they can fly their own planes they may well be alive today.

If we compare the lives of the super-rich to that of a professional with a decent income living with a close-knit family in a fairly comfortable suburban home, the odds are on the latter having a happier life overall and a more satisfying and less stressed-out day-to-day existence.

Hobos, trekking unhurriedly, even aimlessly, down whatever road they randomly pick, with all their earthly possessions hanging on their backs, are more content and at peace with the world than the people in flashy cars whizzing past them.

The farmer who works his field, often with his family, from dawn till sunset, then shares with his loved ones a hard-earned supper, after which they set out on the porch or beneath some tree where he plays an old guitar while his children sing out of tune, is probably sharing the greatest happiness possible in the world.

The old cottage made warm by the loving presence of its occupants is a grander abode than mansions rarely visited by owners who could not make up their minds on which palatial villa to spend the next few days in. It is an undeniable fact that magnificent manors are hardly home to their masters.

So what is the significance of all those castles and sprawling estates? They are just testimonials to the excessive acquisitive powers of their owners who could not thereafter find better ways to make use of the accumulated wealth.

For again, the only way wealth can be manifested is by squandering it. Millions and billions of currency are just long figures in some account records in some banks, unbeknownst to the world at large, until the owners of the funds buy a super yacht or a flashy limousine that will make others aware that the owners can afford to waste so much money.

Is it worth all the effort, a lifetime of struggle, of cheating and scheming, sometimes even committing of crime, making enemies and breaking up of friendships, even kinship relations, sacrificing time and opportunity to be happy with one's family and friends, so that one can accumulate wealth that one can thereafter throw away?

If one has enough on the table, a decent roof over his head, funds for the children's education and a retirement plan to fall back on in his sunset years, then there isn't really much more to ask for. Everything else will just be trimmings, icing on the cake. Should one exert so much effort for cake icing?

In order to bring about a world where most people find happiness, it is imperative that the human psyche be regeared from its present material orientation towards a realization of the truly important and valuable aspects of human existence.

When the rich are content with what they have or even less than that, and ordinary people do not envy them and are satisfied with what is within their reach, then humanity may begin to share the earth's bounty and civilization's blessings on a more equitable, even if not perfectly equal, basis.

RATIONALIZING
MATERIAL
WORTH

Like humanity's obsession with wealth and power, people love or value things in varying degrees of appreciation - some in extremely illogical proportion to their true benefit to the owner. The values placed on different things are, of course, not universal in all cultures, as certain people may place premium value on certain kinds of seashells which would be as precious as ordinary pebbles to people of other regions. But it is almost universal that certain objects or possessions are given value or symbolisms that are not realistic.

Take precious stones. Diamonds may have practical uses, like in the cutting of other diamonds, glass, metals and other hard objects as well as other applications that science may find for them. But they are hardly worth the tremendous sums that they command as expressions of vanity when worn on the neck or head of rich women or the fingers and cuffs of tycoons. The same, of course, holds true with emeralds and rubies.

Gold has many practical and industrial uses but its real commercial value is, like precious stones, as ornamentation. In fact, it has been the symbol of wealth all over the world. Aluminum has many times more utility for modern industry and daily living but it is so much cheaper.

One reason for this discrepancy is the rarity and difficulty of obtaining diamonds and other precious stones, as well as gold. But rarity would not have mattered much if people did not value them so much as symbols of wealth.

Dinosaur fossils are rare, too - much, much rarer - but since no lady would want to wear a tyrannosaurus tooth or a pterodactyl claw for a pendant the intrinsic value of fossils is simply as scientific study objects or as museum displays.

Rarity plus exclusivity of ownership also make a Lamborghini or a Rolls-Royce so much more valuable than a Ford Taurus or a Honda Civic. But if the price of one Lamborghini is equivalent to ten Tauruses or Civics, there simply is no justification for it. In the first place a Lamborghini is less comfortable than a Taurus or a Civic. It could not take as many people as even only one of either.

Perhaps a Rolls-Royce will be more comfortable, but not by much, for a Civic or a Taurus is not exactly a rickety tin can. Oh, yes, the Lambo is twice as fast as a Civic but it cannot go even a quarter of its top speed in the United States. Elsewhere, maybe it can but only for short bursts unless the driver has a death wish.

What about high-priced restaurants? Is the food so much more delicious in five-star restaurants than in common eating places? Is it five times, ten times, twenty times better?

Unless one throws in gold powder along with the pepper, the prices are not anywhere near justified. Only the distinction, the arrogance, of dining where common folk cannot even set foot in makes the difference.. In other words, for the feeling of superiority over ordinary mortals.

But do those trimmings really matter? Do we really care if John F. Kennedy or his wife Jacqueline wore diamond rings? Did it matter if George Washington rode a handsome Arabian stallion or a farm mule to battle?

Surely, Barbra Streisand can walk around in old jeans and a faded shirt, or even go on the concert stage in such a getup and she will still be THE Streisand. Did Pablo Picasso have to drive in a limousine to be the artistic giant he was? Albert Einstein could have gone around wearing a loincloth and he would not have been regarded less of a genius.

Muhammad Ali ended up penniless or at least deeply in debt, but he was, nevertheless, The Greatest. Did anybody talk about or even take notice of who tailored his suit and made his shoes when he made his public appearances?

The world remembers Steven Spielberg's great movies, not whether he goes home to a 100-room mansion or a simple flat in some obscure part of town. William Shakespeare may never have owned a nice carriage to take him to the theater where his plays were staged; really, he may have walked all the way, hopping and crisscrossing his way to avoid puddles made by the London rains. Gandhi may never even have set foot inside an haute cuisine restaurant.

Nelson Mandela spent most of his nights inside a cold and dank prison cell; no, not anything like the presidential suite of a five-star hotel. Ho Chi Minh wore the same clothes as the Vietnamese peasantry. Most modern European royalty try to live in the same style as common citizens. Jordan's King Abdullah II loved to drive his family around aboard a motorcycle with a sidecar, hardly the prescribed mode of transport for a monarch.

The jewelry, expensive cars, designer clothes and all those extravagant objects are the props, the crutches, of those who lack true qualities worth admiring, besides possession of plenty of money.

Does ownership of a collection of antiques make the owner a more brilliant intellectual than his ancestors' genes made him? Oh, and what does the possession of a lock of Elvis Presley's hair, bought for a fortune in some auction, do to someone's persona?

The truly great, the people of substance and achievement, do not need to adorn themselves and their lives with things of artificial value. They only have to be what they are - themselves.

We have to discard the age-old concepts of false values for objects that not only draw away resources from more important things but also make ordinary people covet and wish for objects that would not be truly useful if and when they are obtained.

The factory owner who wants to buy a private jet could put the funds to better use and be better appreciated as a person if he raises the wages of his workers instead. The socialites who bedeck themselves with precious stones could instead set up scholarships for bright but destitute youth, or donate generous sums to research for cures for AIDS, cancer, etc.

So what if we suddenly impoverish De Beers? Or Christian Dior? The jewelry and fashion industries have been fattening themselves on false values, blowing up the vanities of the stupid rich, conjuring a fantasy world that has no true bearing on mankind's existence and society's upliftment.

Why should we glorify and enrich Lamborghini and Ferrari for making impractical, overpriced cars? Why should one wear a Rolex when quartz watches can be just as, or even more, accurate time-keepers?

But wait, surely some people will say: "What about art pieces? Don't they also command fantastic prices, some even cost a fortune, when they do not have commensurate utility and service to the owners?"

Ah, yes. For that matter, would the world have been a more miserable place had Leonardo Da Vinci never painted the Mona Lisa? Would mankind have missed anything if Beethoven did not compose such magnificent symphonies which are played by the highest-paid virtuosos before elite audiences?

The advance of civilization, the triumphs and tragedies of all others who lived and died, would have gone on just he same, right?

Oh, but there is a great big difference. The fantastic prices that some art works and artists command are a recognition of outstanding human talent. They are a measure of the respect accorded certain gifted human beings whose works are a monument to the limitlessness of man's creativity.

What's more, the huge values of these works of art do not usually go to the artists who created them, for they are mostly long dead.

They go to the individuals and organizations that also spent vast amounts to acquire and preserve them.

What about astronomical compensation for nonessential services?

Does Tom Cruise's acting do more benefit to mankind than the work of a farmer growing corn to feed a thousand people? Is tennis legend Roger Federer performing greater service to society than the garbage man who takes away the potential sources of stench and disease?

Or did Michael Jackson deserve the dizzying figures on his recording contracts and advertising deals while millions were starving in Ethiopia not for lack of will to work but because there was drought and they could not coax the soil to yield growth?

Sure, we are able to escape our everyday humdrum existence by the fantasies inspired by Marilyn Monroe, Elizabeth Taylor, Sharon Stone, Clark Gable, Errol Flynn, Sean Connery, Brad Pitt and so many others who come and go. Generations have been thrilled and perhaps will go on swooning over Elvis Presley; we have unforgettable exciting memories of Muhammad Ali's exploits and Michael Jordan's basketball genius.

Really now, would we be less civilized if Mike Tyson never knocked anybody out cold? Or if nobody broke Babe Ruth's homerun record? Would some of us have died if Luciano Pavarotti did not reach such high notes?

Oh, but these people and their worth to the world and humanity cannot be measured in dollars and cents. Their great achievements and the effects of their efforts on many people are either so awesome or so unique that they must be revered or immortalized as epitomes of human excellence. They are inspirations for the world's masses, some even for many generations to come.

How many athletes could approximate Michael Jordan's supreme hardcourt wizardry? He was a joy to behold while in action, countless basketball games were made so exciting and dramatic by his feats. So many moments of His Airness' career remain in the memories of millions of all races and cultures who have been blessed with the opportunity to witness such pure athletic creativity and daring.

Perhaps Mike Tyson's fame, and notoriety, could be considered a sad chapter in the annals of boxing , but during the time he was wearing the heavyweight crown, and even afterwards when he was no longer champion, the world wanted to watch his fights, whether they wanted him to win or to be cut down and humiliated. People paid to see him fight, commercial sponsors scrambled to get advertising mileage from the television coverage of his bouts.

The fabulous royalties that some best-selling authors get from their books represent the number of people they have touched and entertained through their cerebral labors.

Michael Crichton and J. K. Rowling have enthralled countless millions with their fiction and fantasy novels and enriched the minds of so many young people. If they had earned large sums, specially when their books became movies, they were truly worth such, not only to those who invested millions in the projects but to the worldwide audience as well.

Then again, even if the works and services of those gifted personalities command astronomical prices, that fact hardly induces ordinary individuals to wrongdoing. People do not fight tooth and nail, cheat and scheme, to get rich so they can buy a Monet or a Rembrandt. They will do all that, even steal and murder, for a Jaguar, an Aston Martin, or a Beverly Hills house.

Then, too, one did not have to be rich to enjoy Jurassic Park or Harry Potter, or Jordan's greatness, or Sharon Stone's sex-laden movies, nor Frank Sinatra's music. One only had to pay a cheap theater or stadium ticket, or just turn on a television set or a radio. The reason they have made so much money is because they brought pleasure and delight to so many.

They may not have directly fed a hungry mouth with their performances, but they have made millions forget, even for fleeting moments, their misery – some have even inspired and brought hope, even if symbolical or purely fantasy. Of course, many of these superstars also donated both their money and their efforts for the less fortunate of the planet.

Having cleared that up, we go back to the question of putting the true value on things that we use or want to have.

Devaluing diamonds will only damage the very rich who were able to afford them, or those who have tried to emulate the rich by buying them as gifts for their loved ones – but for the latter, both giver and recipient, the intention and the thought that went into the purchase of the gems will remain precious.

Then, too, the jewels and other erstwhile expensive objects that are in the possession of the rich and famous can still be valuable as mementoes of an era when they were highly-prized and –priced, and could still be treasured as heirlooms or antiques.

Heirlooms are also precious and even priceless, but mainly only to the owners – other people will not envy them for that and surely not murder them to steal the objects.

Designer clothes, previously bought, if they are truly beautiful will remain thus even if they will no longer be in vogue. In fact, they may even be more valuable or memorable if they will be the last thousand-dollar creations of Versace or whoever. At any rate, people can be gorgeous in anything if they are truly well-shaped and have bearing and move gracefully. No level of haute couture will make a misshapen and awkward person elegant.

Too, you can have the most expensive Gucci leather bags and shoes and be ignored if you are really not somebody important or are not worth talking to. You may have arrived at the party in the most shiny Rolls-Royce but remember that only the doorman and the host (if he is at the lobby or door to welcome guests) saw it. Inside the ballroom, it is your worth as a person that will count.

LOVE AND SEX

In the modern world, particularly in western and other secular societies, love – romantic love, that is – is a very important factor in the lives of men and women, generally more important for the latter. To individuals in such milieus, to live lives without love, or, worse, to live with mates they do not love, is as close to hell as one can be or at least would be a meaningless, joyless existence.

Yet, in many countries and societies in other parts of the world, romantic love is not a factor, is even a non-thing. Where men and women are paired off to be husbands and wives by agreement of parents or by arrangement of matchmakers, men and women do not even have a notion of romantic love. They are mated, have a family and share a life till death do they part, or where divorce is allowed, till such happens.

That was the practice in most of the world in earlier times. In India, China, and other ancient societies, women, and sometimes even the men, did not have much choice or say on whom they will be paired off for life. Elders did it for them, or brides were sold off to rich men, or fathers had to pay dowries to have their daughters find husbands and get them off their hands. There was almost no possibility for romance.

The truth is, even if romantic love is so glorified in stories like that about Romeo and Juliet, in the western world many centuries ago, romance hardly ever happened to most people of their time. Yes, not even in the time of Romeo and Juliet.

People almost never got to intimately know those who are not of their station in life, nor even those of their own station but not of the same village or town. One stayed in one's village, among one's peers. One had to marry someone from that very small circle of acquaintances, in many instances even one's kin, cousins or aunts or uncles.

Even when young people were not of a mind to get married, their parents usually pressured them to get hitched, to get them off their households. A maiden had to be married off before she becomes too old for marrying, like a reject, and to lessen the burden on the family cupboard. The same goes for the young man, unless he helps work the farm but then he is better off with a wife to wash his clothes, cook his food and do womanly things that his mother used to do for him, even as he still helps with the farm.

There was not much choice in those instances. Often, a young person would be lucky to find an available partner. Should there be more young maidens than bachelors in the village, or vice versa, then there would be a problem. Sometimes, a wandering traveler would be cajoled into taking a village maiden with him to wife. Or when there is a paucity of maidens, a visiting female relative of some villager will be besieged by suitors, no matter her looks or life circumstances.

In colonial times, when men first sailed out to settle in lands claimed by colonizing powers, they often sent for brides from their homelands and whatever the shape and size and countenance of a bride that was sent, she was welcomed. The brides were mostly daughters of destitute families who were only too happy to have one less mouth to feed. There was no romance in those liaisons. One took whatever was available.

Yet, all those people survived and multiplied, and they must have found some degree of happiness somehow and thrived, for many of today's Americans, Australians and Latin Americans are their descendants – even if, as has been pointed out, very few of their ancestors really got to pair off with their own chosen loves.

The culture of romantic love between couples, whether for keeps or for temporary affairs, was made possible mainly by the industrial revolution of the eighteenth and nineteenth centuries and was further boosted by the rapid technological developments from the twentieth.

The industrial revolution that saw the creation of machines and the establishment of factories took people away from farms and family-based cottage industries and brought them to work in the cities or boom towns. Men and women from far-flung places came together where work was available and thereby met more of the opposite sex than they could ever had hoped to see and know in their villages and hamlets. Suddenly, there were choices. Romeos could meet Juliets. Cinderellas could meet and choose from, well, charming guys.

The more technology developed, specially in the mode and speed of transportation, the more mobile people became and the more from the opposite sex they came to know. Of course, with so many choices, the chances and temptations for infidelity also multiplied.

One no longer had to stick to one homely wife in a village where there were few other women and all were spoken for. There were so many women, and even men who were already married could find opportunities for illicit liaisons. For the women, it was the same.

Thus, romance came to be. And it came to be part of man-woman relationships. In our own times, with the tremendous leaps in communications systems, individuals can now surf for possible partners on the internet. In a few more years, who knows what new possibilities will come about?

So what is this thing called love? It apparently did not exist before, or did not exist for so many people. It could not be an inherent emotion or need or whatever of humans, for countless generations flourished and propagated the species without the benefit of the thing.

Let us not confuse love in the romantic context with love for one's offspring, or family, including the mate (wife or husband) that has developed through bonding and familial loyalty. Love for family members may be an instinct, as it also exists in many animals. We think the loyalty of the dove or the wolf to its mate is romantic but it is actually instinctive as they are all fixated on their particular mates and usually would not even take cognizance of other possible mates, once they have one of their own.

Even those people of today who are supposed to be in love are almost never really in love in the textbook, or shall we say pocketbook, sense.

It is not unusual for men to court and be involved with several women at once. They may prefer one woman above all the rest, but chances are she is the most physically attractive, the prettiest among the "harem" or the one who, for some reason, gives the man the greatest pleasure.

Or a guy may court one woman alone but once he gets jilted he will immediately court another, immediately forgetting or casting away the memory of his "first love" or his "one true love."

A woman, who is supposed to be less promiscuous than the male, may seem to be faithfully devoted to her boyfriend or fiance, or even husband, until some really attractive or dashing fellow sweeps her off her feet and her undying love switches over to the new guy. Of course, if nobody attractive and dashing enough comes along, or no such fellow wants to sweep her off her feet, we assume that she is truly and eternally in love with her one and only. But that is only because no dashing guy ever crossed her path.

People, specially women, must be disabused of the notion of true love, particularly of the false hope that somewhere out there is the "right one" for everyone. No, there is no "Mr. Right" or "Ms. Right" – one must be thankful if one finds a partner that is suitable, and even that is purely accidental.

True love is a fallacy from the instant of flirtation or courtship. Beautiful women are besieged by suitors, ugly women are not, of course. It is not love but physical attraction that drives men. If some men go for women who are not attractive it is simply because they know they cannot hope to get the attractive ones.

On the reverse side of the coin, handsome men, or rich and powerful men, or men who exude masculinity, get a lot of women. It may seem like a riddle why there are men who meet a number of supposedly desirable standards – decency, manners, pleasant appearance and personality, college education, etc. – yet could not seem to attract women. Well, not really.

It is not the nice guys women go for but men who are "macho" in any of several ways – money, power, status, strong personality, also looks (but the last does not count among the top reasons in real life, only when the guy is a movie star or a pop singer, but being such is usually sexual attraction enough even without good looks).

Nice guys - the hero types – only win the women in pocketbook romances and in movies. In reality, the bad guys even usually get more women than the nice and proper accountant or dentist next door.

No romantic love in those realities. Sex appeal is the primeval cause. That is why even when women have the right and opportunity to make choices, they usually don't fall for the kind of men their mothers would have wanted for them, or that are idealized in pulp romances and soap operas.

How many individuals can say they have found their true love? Well, married couples can claim so, but they are really lying most of the time. Almost every married person has missed out on a "true love" somewhere in the past. Or secretly knows he/she never got to meet the "right one" and just has to make the best out of his/her life with the partner he/she got.

What many mistake for true love, or being deeply in love, is actually only a very strong attraction to a certain person, which, if the feeling is reciprocated, may take on a more permanent character as it evolves into what anthropologists and psychologists call "pair bonding". When a pair has bonded strongly then people assume that the pair are truly and deeply and faithfully in love with one another. But it could probably be likened only to the bonding of doves and wolves, although it is possible that human bonding is not as strong because such "faithfulness" is less prevalent and is definitely not general among the human species.

This notion of a man's, or a woman's, love having to be eternal and meant for only one object of affection may seem a harmless fantasy to those who will admit that it is not a true emotion. But it is not harmless fantasy because many people, specially women, believe it to be eternal and universal truth. That misconception has caused countless emotional, physical and legal conflicts since it became widespread belief.

Partners demand that their mates remain faithful and profess that they are, when it is very easy for them to be attracted to others and succumb to temptation. Then relationships come to a head, marriages and families break up; sometimes, nay, oftentimes, violence takes place.

Domestic troubles arising from infidelity are the most painful of all, particularly to the "wronged" partner and leave the longest-lasting scars in the psyche. Naturally, children suffer a lot whenever their parents quarrel or divorce or separate and studies show that children from broken homes are prone to be unhappy and relive their parents' mistakes or react in the reverse direction in a manner that may defy common reason.

People in societies where monogamy is the prescribed custom are the only ones who are afflicted with this problem. Fidelity as a requisite for married life on the part of the man is an artificial burden. The problems that arise from the violation of that requirement do not affect non-monogamous societies.

In Muslim societies and other cultures where men are allowed polygamous relationships or to keep concubines, there is greater harmony within the family, which are even extended ones where the man's offspring by several women are raised together with all the wives nurturing the children.

Men in Biblical times had many wives, and there is no account of any man who encountered trouble with any of his wives because of his "infidelity" for it was not infidelity from their viewpoint in those days. Fidelity of the male is a false demand of recent culture, not inherent in the nature of the human animal.

Oh, and what about the fidelity of the human female? Perhaps it was also not inherent at the start. As has been observed in our closest relatives - the higher apes - females, though supposedly the "property" of the alpha male, often engage in sex with other males when the alpha male is not around. Of course, male apes, alpha or not, are polygamous and humans most probably are simply behaving according to instincts inherent in all primates.

Many women have been unfaithful all throughout human history and, most certainly, since the dawn of time. Countless unattached women play the field, jumping from one man's arms to another's without pangs of guilt nor trace of shame.

But most married or attached women remain sexually faithful to their men, and have been so since the figurative time of Adam and Eve. The reason must be the need of the human female to be protected and supported by the male in raising offspring since the human infant requires so many years of nurturing before it becomes capable of surviving by itself. Sexual exclusivity has been the reward of the man for his care for his mate and their progeny.

Perhaps it is most fortunate that the human male is by nature polygamous and, in the early stages of civilization, such instinct had not been inhibited. The human race could not have survived if men had the faithfulness or fixation with only one mate that wolves and doves have.

The human male was combative and presumably engaged in group wars from the dawn of time, either for right to abundant food sources or territory or both. Males would be injured or even killed in encounters with rival groups. Even if the ratio of males to females in a group began at a perfect 1:1 the conflicts the males figured in constantly decreased their number and thus left their mates without reproductive partners. If the surviving males did not take the widows as secondary wives, the tribe's population will be diminished and possibly be wiped out after several skirmishes.

As man developed better weapons and became more efficient at killing or maiming his enemies, this danger was greatly increased, and would probably have resulted in certain demise of large groups or races because there had been many times in history when all the males of one tribe or kingdom had been massacred.

Fortunately for those females, and the human species, the conquering males usually mated with the conquered females, either as concubines, sexual slaves or even true wives. Otherwise those tribes and their genes would have been lost forever.

With disease and other natural disasters also taking their toll, along with infant mortality and female childbirth deaths, the species would surely have been teetering on the brink of extinction.

That the human male possessed the urge to mate with more than one female was the only factor that allowed the species to continue propagating and eventually multiplying to be among the most successful species on the planet.

Women, of course, are also capable of consorting with more than one male partner but that does not really help in increasing the population as a woman will normally only produce one offspring at a time regardless of the number of males she had sex with.

The polygamous nature of men has been gradually kept in check in the last two millennia in many societies as customs, religious tradition and laws evolved to increase a father's obligations to his wives and offspring. In those societies, even when not expressly forbidden by law, it became a great burden for men to maintain more than one family, except for the very rich ones. But even for the very rich ones, the laws on inheritance and apportionment of property often discouraged many wives and children as it resulted in dispersal of property and, therefore, diminished social power for families.

The instinct for polygamous relationship, however, even when forbidden by law, religion and custom, still remained and many men, throughout history, engaged in multiple sexual relationships, temporary and otherwise. That most men, given the chance, will play Don Juan is accepted as a fact of nature – and not always with disgust or disfavor, for lady killers are envied by men and desired by many women.

The human male's sexual philandering, in most liberal societies of modern times, is thus largely tolerated and actually regarded, if tacitly, as a sign of virility and even an extension, or manifestation, of the successful and powerful man's personality.

Feminists may insist that females have the right to more than one partner if such right is allowed men. After all, many women of today, particularly in developed countries, no longer need a man's help in raising a child. That may be so, but the realities of social existence even in this day and age work against women who have multiple sexual relationships.

For one thing, if a woman who has more than one partner gets pregnant, the father's identity will be uncertain. If she wanted to ask for financial support from the father, unless the men she got involved with will agree to undergo DNA examination to find out, it will be almost impossible to assign responsibility. But even if the father can be identified, the main burden of raising the child will be with the woman. She will be left holding the proverbial bag, with a child in it.

In America and other developed societies where women are on nearly equal footing as men in holding jobs and careers the woman who is a single parent will still be in a tight situation trying to raise a child while struggling to earn money.

In less developed countries where women are not very well educated and prepared to make a living, this will be a major disaster for herself and her family.

Like it or not, we rarely see men acting as single parents of children born out of wedlock. After all, the child will develop inside the woman's body and she will deliver it and most probably be stuck with it. Until society evolves into that stage where babies are developed in test tubes or artificial wombs in a laboratory and are taken care of by state institutions from birth, women will be saddled with the burden of offspring.

Even supposing that a woman with multiple partners and relationships can avoid getting pregnant, she will still have to cope with unwanted male sexual advances as many men will not meekly accept rejection by someone who gives in to so many others; thus she will be inviting, albeit unwittingly, rape and violent reactions from injured male pride.

Unless a woman is a Cynthia Luster or a Cindy Rothrock, she will always need the protection of a man. Women without a husband or lover or a male family member to defend her against aggressive suitors, stalkers, and other male, or even female, abusers, very often end up with traumatic experiences from the wild world out there.

She can get mugged, raped, harassed, harangued, robbed and whatnot simply because a woman alone appears quite helpless, and in many instances really is so, against physical and even psychological and emotional attacks. Things that are usually not attempted or wrought on men are more easily and usually inflicted on women, specially single, unprotected ones.

Even hookers who are abused by their pimps are often better off with a regular abuser-protector than striking out on their own and falling prey to so many potential abusers.

In the area of sexual activities, at least, women could not be truly equal to men or attempt to imitate male practices, even if they had similar inclinations as men. It is a rare sexually-liberated woman that really plays the field who can honestly say she has not encountered an unpleasant situation in connection with her sexual adventures as a direct result of her gender.

Only the gold-digging woman can be said to end up ahead in the man-woman sexual exchanges but in many cases it is not really a triumph for the woman as she most probably had to give her body to the man in exchange for material gain, which is just a quid pro quo. If the man is very rich, he may feel he got a bargain for whatever fortune he parted with to have sex with the woman, if he desired her that much and got his libido satiated in the process.

Going back to the matter of love, there is a saying that "Man gives love to get sex, woman gives sex to get love." That is only partially true, because in most instances a man isn't giving real love to get sex, but only feigns love. So the woman is at the short end of the bargain because the sex she gives is real while the love she gets is not.

Going back to the subject of true mating relationships, many, if not most, men are able to fulfill the roles expected of them by society as family providers, husbands to wives and fathers to offspring. Such men may have bonded well with their mates and/or felt strong attachment to their children. This does not mean that those men do not possess the polygamous urge, only that the urge has been subordinated to paternal instinct and social responsibility.

It is most important for individuals to have a better and more realistic understanding of the relationships that transpire between men and women to avoid unhappiness, disappointment and frustration. The importance of love and sex in the lives of individuals does not comprise only the immediate and direct effects on the particular individuals involved but also on their offspring, relatives, friends, even their professions, their community and society as a whole.

Governments, corporations and society in general will benefit greatly if the individuals that compose them are each more emotionally stable and well-settled in their personal lives. On the other hand, it will be very risky, in this day and age and state of technology, if unstable or emotionally-stressed individuals should hold the power to unleash nuclear war or delete all-important programs in a network of computers.

The reality of more individuals suffering emotional and mental distress in sexually-liberated societies can be seen in the number of suicides, psychiatric patients and psychiatrists, as well as the consumption of Prozac and Valium in those societies as compared to the more conservative ones where man-woman relationships are more stable due to cultural and legal strictures.

To prevent women from asserting their rights to sexual freedom, however, will no longer be tolerated in secular and modern societies even if such restriction is specifically meant to protect them and stabilize people's lives. It will be seen as chauvinistic and oppressive.

To balance it, men may be likewise restricted and prevented from giving expression to their polygamous tendencies but that will be harder to do since the human male's instincts have not yet evolved to conform with recent realities. Men now rarely fight wars on an "all-who-could-bear-arms" basis but they still want to grab all women in sight.

Further, to restrict sexual freedom for either gender may be seen as a return to the dark ages when sex was generally looked upon as sinful and dirty and meant only for procreation. Modern man, and even woman, has come to regard and treat sex as an important source of pleasure and among the blessings of life, not just a duty or urge for the propagation of the species.

Further still, the invasion and proliferation of global communications and cultural information into even the most conservative communities had set off a consciousness of the freedoms enjoyed by people, including women, in modern countries and it is probable that people everywhere, including women, will demand, one way or another, the same freedoms.

Naturally, women who are sexually liberated will have to sacrifice something in return, like the security of being a wife, which may be more important in the long run and in the final analysis for a woman. True, a liberated woman can also marry and become a wife but it is not the same as being a wife for a conservative woman in a conservative society.

Somehow, sexually liberated women's status as wives seem shaky and temporary, and their husbands will most probably not be strongly committed to the union, too, knowing that their wives are not very sexually attached to them - not being the first and only man ever for the woman - and may even find the husbands inadequate compared to former partners.

There is a difference, of course, between engaging in premarital sex or sex in a cohabiting relationship and casual sex. Men readily engage in casual sex, or sex for entertainment, which includes picking up strange women or engaging prostitutes.

Not very many women, it may be presumed, engage in casual sex. Sex outside marriage for most women is usually still an integral part of some form of relationship, even if it is only friendship. Or if there is no sort of relationship yet in existence, it is usually with the hope of developing one in the process of engaging in sex. True, some women may pick up casual partners in singles bars but the majority of the "weaker gender" are not so bold and adventurous or very casual about sex.

Besides the woman's need for male protection and the man's need for domestic attention and their common longing for a constant sexual partner, there is the need for opposite sex companionship, which is separate from the sex act and may last to their extreme old age "till death do they part".

For those couples who have found devoted care and solace with one another, life together will be one long comfortable and blissful sharing. This is the ideal male-female relationship, whether within marriage or as cohabiting partners (although if they are so compatible and there are no legal impediments, then such couples probably would have gotten married somewhere along the way). The problem is, such fortunate unions are not very common in modern society.

With modern life so complex - what with financial and material concerns cluttering up emotional interchanges between couples, growing children becoming problems in so many different ways, careers requiring life-changing decisions - husbands and wives or cohabiting partners have to contend with so many rocky obstacles on the road to working out a viable and permanent relationship.

Men and women in so-called liberated societies must learn to accept that the ideal relationship may not be attainable by just any couple, that one may not find his or her "soulmate" in the person he or she is attracted to and therefore they must adjust their expectations on the sort of relationship they are to have.

Society and culture and social institutions must also adapt to such realities. These are no longer the days when the farmer's son takes the first, perhaps the only, village maiden to wife and they live together in a cottage and raise children to work the farm with them, and their children will live the same way in a never-ending "sunrise-sunset" cycle.

Now we never know when the farmer's or business executive's daughter will get pregnant by some man who would not or could not marry her or whom she herself does not want to marry. Or when the bus driver or the computer programmer will walk out of his home and shack up with another woman, leaving wife and children like some pieces of unwanted clothes.

People in "liberated" societies must do away with the fantasies and fallacies concerning sexual relationships and calibrate their attitudes and desires according to the diverse and continually mutating social and personal realities of individuals in the increasingly complex world that is evolving around us.

Then, of course, social institutions must forge and adopt new ways to regulate as well as protect the rights of everyone based on the developing situations in human interrelationships. Some of the laws delineating the rights and responsibilities of conjugal partners and parents may have become obsolete or no longer applicable to the changing behavior, attitudes and ways of life of modern humans.

Too, people in less liberal societies who want to adopt western, or modern, ways must be made aware of the pitfalls and dangers of the new attitudes and practices. They may find that their old ways – the solid nuclear family, definite roles of the sexes, etc. – are better, given their specific wants and needs and expectations in life. Or they may benefit from retaining some of their old ways and making adjustments here and there as they evolve a new social environment for themselves and their future descendants.

FREEDOM VS. CONFORMITY AND SECURITY

The modern person desires and considers a matter of right such lofty and noble ideals as personal freedom, security of person and property, equal and unlimited opportunity, dignity of the individual and so many other abstract values which were completely alien and beyond the comprehension of most people who had lived a century or two before.

Individual freedom, which is regarded as the pillar of all other individual rights, is regarded not only as the greatest gift a human being is heir to by nature of his or her humanity, but the engine which has driven the most creative and productive powers of the best human talents to soar to heights that brought about mankind's march to an ever-changing, ever-progressing world.

Before the age of industrialization which ushered in the close and multitudinal intermingling of people of all sorts of origin, station and ability, majority of the members of society were at the bottom rung and were too preoccupied with the struggle for survival to think of abstract ideas like individual freedom.

On top of that, they were too ignorant and too economically helpless to be able to handle individual freedom. For freedom is not simply a license to do as one pleases or go where he feels an itch to be. It has to be tempered by responsibility and obligation.

One must not do an act that will harm or offend another, so a person exercising his freedom must ensure that whatever he does will not encroach on the rights of others, or if it does it must be within the bounds of accepted law or social custom.

If he wants to cut the limb of a tree that he feels to be a potential threat to his house should it fall during a storm but whose trunk and roots are on his neighbor's side of the fence, he has to ask permission from the neighbor who, for all intents and purposes, is the tree's owner. If the adjoining land was public domain he would probably have to ask leave from the community authorities.

If he feels like singing on top of his voice he could only do so if it does not annoy or bother his neighbors. Should he want to pass through a property enclosed by a fence, or that which is known to be privately owned, he should not take one step without first asking leave of the landlord.

In the dawn of civilization primitive men surrendered part of their freedom in order to establish order and harmony among themselves within the group they belonged to. They recognized the authority of the tribal council or chieftain and/or the shaman or whoever wielded power or supposedly possessed spiritual wisdom. In vital aspects of their communal life, they exercised no freedom of choice and submitted to the leaders' wishes or commands.

As civilized society became larger and the living conditions of people became more complicated, people became specialized in their various roles in communal life and their individual status became stratified.

The complex stratification resulted in a corresponding complex variation in degrees of loss of freedom, similar to the pecking order of a large flock of birds kept together in one super enclosure.

Leaders of large communities in the past strove to establish control over their constituents by restricting as much of their individual freedom as they can effectively keep in check. Thus despots arose; some truly intending to use their powers over the people they dominated for the good of those people and the community or state, but others only to stifle dissent against their rule.

Nevertheless, in the early days of civilization and up to the Middle Ages - or perhaps even until before the nineteenth and twentieth centuries - communities, kingdoms and nations led by rulers with an iron hand usually succeeded in subjugating those whose citizens were not so obedient to their leaders who were more liberal, lax and, therefore, in most instances, also weak.

This principle was best exemplified in armies, for soldiers that obeyed their general without question, even if the odds seemed unfavorable, had a better chance to triumph over those who refused or hesitated to do the bidding of their commander.

Through most of history the kingdoms and empires that rose above their rivals were led and ruled by strong leaders and peopled by obedient citizens who either believed in the righteousness of their empires' cause or the divine mandate of their monarchs.

Tyrants and all sorts of kings may have been deposed but there always remained a ruling class that controlled power over the masses which had to continually accede to the edicts of whoever held authority.

True democracy could not have flourished prior to the development of technology, when freedom of enterprise and unfettered experimentation with ideas fueled industry which became the backbone of the strength of nations in place of military conquest and colonization. Thus the United States of America was very fortunate to have been born along with the Industrial Revolution, otherwise the young republic could have been a failure and fallen into the fate of other vast nations that disintegrated into fiefdoms under various warlords.

Many dreamers of today fantasize of a world without government and bureaucracies, but that, needless to say, is an impossible dream - yes, one of the few things we have to concede to be impossible. Modern man, as a social animal, could not exist without some form of government and official control. It has been said time and again by the greatest thinkers that any form of government is better than no government.

Indeed, we cannot but suppose that government, even in its most primitive form, has always existed in human, and even pre-human, society. Most primates, particularly those that are native to Africa, are social animals that are held together by a leader, usually the highest-ranking male, and are subject to a hierarchy.

There are upheavals in the societies of our primate relatives but eventually they settle under the rule of dominant members. The same has always been true of human societies and communities that survived through various stretches of time.

In the currently prevailing attitude of most civilized people, the ideal leader will be a benevolent, kindly fatherlike, or motherlike, figure who does not rule but rather cajoles and convinces, whose words and visions inspire and move all constituents to do the right thing and follow the right path. Instead of dominating, the leader will be friendly and heroic, even saintly.

Alas, such a person cannot be a leader, unless the constituents are meek, blindly pious faithful of some religious sect held together and in thrall by their common spiritual belief.

True, there have been some very charismatic leaders in history who had the gift, or magic, of persuasiveness, who had no need to intimidate others for whatever it is they wanted or wanted done. But societies and nations do not always find such people available for their leadership; and, if there should be one or some, they often have rivals and enemies who would do anything, not the least assassination, to prevent them from assuming or retaining power.

Of course, that holds true for any kind of potential or actual leader. There are always ambitious and covetous pretenders who want the positions of power for themselves. Too, no decision or action made by any leader will be universally beneficial to everyone affected by said decision or action and he will therefore make enemies whatever he does.

If a leader should order the creation and distribution of an elixir that would give eternal life to all the people, it will be foolish to assume that everyone would thence be happy.

The coroners and operators of funeral homes and cemeteries will not want death to die. Such an elixir would presumably also eradicate disease, or at least render diseases harmless because they could no longer kill, so there will be no need to cure them. That would thus make workers of the medical profession and owners of medical and pharmaceutical institutions bitter enemies of the leader who would render them useless and without means of livelihood.

There would be no paucity of reasons for all kinds of leaders to displease and alienate certain members and sectors of their constituency and so leaders, in order to be effective, have to be tough and resolute, sometimes despotic and ruthless.

Leaders normally survive making harsh decisions when such adversely affect only a small part of their constituency. Their problems arise when a large segment, or even the majority, of the people will be suffering to some degree because of a particular decision, policy or law; or if powerful interests or sectors, even though in the minority, are adversely affected. Then leaders may have to rule with an iron hand and resort to drastic measures to implement said decision, policy or law.

Such leaders could not be countenanced in a society where the individual freedom of its members allows them to reject and disobey their leaders and even remove them from their posts. So how does a leader in this kind of society handle situations that arouse the disapproval and resistance of a large or powerful segment of that society?

In most instances, such leaders, having no choice but to stay their hand, allow the status quo to linger, until such time that the situation they wanted to remedy goes out of control and becomes too harmful for the people in general that they could take appropriate action with the acceptance even of those who opposed them at the beginning or without further legitimate opposition..

But there may be situations where leaders could not wait for matters to worsen, when to wait and be indecisive would be irreparable or even fatal.

For instance, a country's people may have been so used to rice as their staple food and could not produce enough for their own consumption. The government and other institutions will have to import the commodity but it is a time when their foreign currency reserves are running so low and food imports will eat away money intended for medicines and other vital needs. The country's land can produce maize more abundantly to provide for the people's nourishment but the people refuse to replace their staple food because they find maize distasteful or difficult to chew and digest.

To allow the people to continue with their age-old eating habits would mean to do without other equally, or more, important needs. The leader has to act as he sees fit, even if his constituents belittle the dangers they are being warned of, thinking that the need for medicines may not come or not to the degree the leader foresees.

We could see that freedom is not always positive. For the free individual does not always think and act correctly. There are many instances when individuals, entire communities and nations, have to be guided, even coerced, into following the right path.

There have also been, and will be, situations when free-thinking and -acting individuals are convinced by unscrupulous charlatans into doing things that are not to the best interests of society or are morally and legally wrong, like rioting and rebelling against duly constituted government not because that government is overly oppressive but because the charlatans want to grab power for themselves and managed to delude masses of people into believing they are the righteous would-be saviors who will solve the people's myriad problems.

Or the manipulators may not want something so momentous but only want government to change a certain policy that is inimical to their interests. Glib talkers can hoodwink masses of people, highlighting what is important and advantageous to their purposes and passing over or even downright belying what is not.

On the personal level, it must be considered that not every person is prepared and able, or desires, to exercise individual freedom.

For the exercise of individual freedom entails making individual decisions on practically every aspect of one's existence. Not only does a person have to think about so many things, he or she must make the right choices; otherwise, he or she will suffer the consequences.

Many, probably most, people are not intelligent enough to make the right choices all, or most, of the time; or even in just the most critical situations. For that matter, even the most intelligent, well-educated and –informed people often make wrong choices.

Again, there is also the matter of responsibility. A free individual who can decide which way to go and what to do must be responsible for the consequences and effects of his decisions.

A person driving a car who sees a large truck closing fast from behind may choose to switch to another lane to avoid the possibility of getting rearended by the huge vehicle and in the process sideswipes a station wagon on the lane he swerves into, causing injuries or even death of some of the wagon's passengers.

If the driver is weak-hearted, he may be so stricken with fear and guilt that he may not want to drive again. In the first place, the weak-hearted person may never have tried to drive at all, even if it is his right to do so.

In everyday life, the individual has to make countless such sudden decisions, some of no moment, others of extreme importance. Not only is the individual's intelligence and judgment taxed with countless problems big and small, his courage and fortitude are also continually put to the test.

It is for this reason that certain, and not very few, individuals give up their freedom of choice. Most people are not aware of it when they do, however. For they surrender their freedom of choice indirectly, subtly and unconsciously – by heeding the advice of others, or following the example of people they consider their betters, instead of thinking for themselves. They would rather be sheep being shepherded and stay in the security of the fold.

Even rioting masses could actually be such people, seemingly expressing their anger and hatred as an exercise of freedom, when, in fact, they are just giving in to the herd mentality, doing reckless things because some leaders told them to and their fellows are doing the same. They are just conforming, afraid to stand up for their own feelings and beliefs. Sometimes, too, for the intellectually weak, the fact that everybody else is doing one thing validates the act and convinces them that it is the right thing to do.

Another instance of unwanted or detrimental freedom was experienced by many of the black and colored slaves that were set free by Abraham Lincoln's Great Emancipation. The former slaves felt lost and helpless when allowed, and forced, to fend for themselves and live as free men and women. Many only knew the unchanging regularity of their life as slaves, when they were fed and housed by their masters, without the problem of trying to provide for themselves the things they needed.

It may have been a tedious, monotonous existence they led as slaves, but it was safe and secure. They knew what they have to do the next day and the day after that, and they knew they will have food and a roof over their heads the next day and the day after that. No, they did not have to battle with the unknown and fearful challenges of the big, wide world they were so unfamiliar with.

It may be posited that today's people are not slaves, or former slaves, who are coming out into a strange, hostile world. Perhaps not slaves, but unprepared to meet the struggles of everyday existence just the same; through ignorance, poverty, natural lack of intelligence, weakness of character, a myriad causes for failure.

In many socialist and communist countries like the Soviet Union, East Germany, Poland and Romania, where the people have been living under government-controlled economies which they later overturned by popular people's uprisings, the newly liberated citizens suddenly found that they were not prepared to fend for themselves in a free-market society and there were, and still are, sizeable sectors longing to return to "the bad old days" when they had less, or practically non-existent, personal freedom but had steady jobs and comparatively secure lives.

Here we can also look at the tendency of many people, specially young ones, to dress a certain way, walk, talk and act in a peculiar manner – supposedly as an expression of their generation or class, to distinguish themselves from other groups like their elders or their younger siblings. But when the fashion that is in vogue becomes so widespread, the opposite purpose may actually be that which is in operation.

Instead of assuming a certain stance, manner and style to proclaim individuality and identity as a group, the individual may be acting to CONFORM to that group, to merge and lose himself into the crowd and avoid standing out and getting noticed.

Probably a very vivid though heartrending example of this tendency was provided by the Afghan women after the Taliban were driven out of power in Afghanistan by the American-led forces.

Freed from the Taliban edict that women should wear face masks called burqa when going out in public, many of them chose to keep wearing those hideous symbols of gender repression. It was apparent many of them did not have the courage to show their faces – themselves - to their neighbors and countrymen.

They preferred to be incognito, obviously feeling more secure in their anonymity. They were given freedom to come out of their shells and display their identity; but they were not ready, or confident enough, to savor that liberty.

For many of the world's teeming masses, freedom is not only a double-edged sword that cuts both ways, but something that they could not really enjoy for they lack the abilities to make use of it.

Freedom, that noblest of human ideals, is not always a good thing.

CRIME AND EVIL: DISEASES OF ALL SOCIETIES

Since man became a social animal, he has committed crimes on his fellowmen, even his brothers and sisters. The biblical story of Cain and Abel illustrates the basal and ingrained nature of crime in the human psyche.

All over the world, in nations rich and poor, in all kinds of social structures and religious cultures, people commit crimes on property and person.

Here we have to separate what is commonly called sexual crimes - meaning rape, sexual abuse or exploitation, polygamy, adultery, pedophilia, immodest or lewd behavior, and the like. There are several reasons why such crimes must not be classified along with those involving theft and violence.

One, there may be complex psychological roots and impulses behind many, maybe most, of them that only extensive psychiatric investigations can identify.

Two, there are cultures and societies where things like rape are not considered crimes, where even women who are victims take it as some sort of sport, particularly among some primitive tribes.

Then, there are cultures where sexual exploitation of girls from poor families is accepted as inevitable, and even desired by those very girls and their families when such assures them of food and lodging, sometimes even payment to the parents.

Also, there are some cultures where rape, instead of being a crime or a violation of women, is regarded as just punishment for women whose behavior deviate from the norms of their society. Too, some cultures, the male-dominated ones, regard rape or forcible or coercive sex as the right or privilege of men over those women who are in their household or are otherwise beholden to them.

We normally or generally look at crimes as violations of a society's laws and rules of behavior that result in injury to others and must be punished in accordance with established codes. In all communities and societies, there are penal systems instituted to deal with most, if not all, harmful or unlawful conduct.

Theft and crimes involving property and material possessions are not always driven by need because even the very rich steal. Nor of inability to attain their desires, because sometimes rich people are caught stealing objects they could easily buy, in the same way some men, who could pay the most beautiful women to submit to their pleasure, commit rape, sometimes on women not at all pretty.

Violent crimes are not always a result of anger for sometimes heinous deeds are driven by sick, sadistic urges. Bullies derive pleasure from inflicting harm, physical or emotional and psychological, on those they perceive as weak and likely victims.

Crimes against property will be more easily prevented and solved because they can be called logical crimes. Logical because they are done for a definite objective – material gain – in the same way commercial endeavors are engaged in for profit.

It will thus be easier to guard and defend the obvious targets, money and things of value - and find who took them, in case.

Fraud, bribery and extortion, which are perpetrated with some degree of cooperation from the victim, may be even easier to prove and prosecute as there is at least one witness – the victim – unless the victim is killed afterwards, which would be another, and worse, crime – murder, the greatest crime against person.

Crimes against persons, particularly the violent sort, are much more difficult to prevent, and sometimes resolve and prosecute. In most instances outbursts of violence are sudden and unpredictable. Even if it is between established enemies, one cannot always accurately discern how long they will just engage in vocal tirades and argument, or perhaps silent animosity; and foresee if and when the antagonists will physicalize their hostility.

Sometimes, violence erupts between people who do not even know each other, and therefore have no prior ground for confrontation. Or they may indeed belong to opposing factions but are not personally familiar with one another and were drawn into an adversarial situation only by virtue of their group affiliations, as in gang wars.

Violent crimes are therefore difficult to prevent when they are either spontaneous and unexpected; and difficult to solve because, unless the guilty parties are apprehended immediately, it is nearly impossible to pinpoint their identities as there are no prior conflicts between the opposite sides.

Deliberate and premeditated crimes are also difficult to prevent because the perpetrators will do everything within their mental and physical, as well as mechanical and technological, capabilities to enact them when least expected; and difficult to solve as the criminals will also employ all means to mislead investigators.

But the problems in preventing both crimes against property and against persons can be overcome, mainly by making it almost impossible to escape justice in a preponderant majority of cases.

Where direct and active prevention is possible, such can be done with the help of technology now available and some being developed. Where direct prevention is not yet feasible then the very overwhelming probability of successful prosecution will be both retribution and deterrent.

Yes, there is a way to make successful prosecution of most crimes a probability. But be patient, please, dear reader – that will come in another chapter.

DIVERSITY AND CONFLICT OF INTERESTS BETWEEN NATIONS AND PEOPLES

The general aspirations of individuals, peoples and nations may be the same the world over, but the paths to their similar goals are not always the same. In many instances, they run counter to each other. Or they may choose the same roads but not everyone can traverse said roads as there is not enough room. Or they are after the same pot of gold, which is actually an inevitability.

Just as practically every person wants to be rich or get richer, or gain superiority over his fellows, so do all nations and peoples want to dominate and grab the largest shares in world commerce and industry. But most countries and peoples do not have the resources and technology to compete with the Americans, Japanese, Germans and Chinese.

The industrialized nations may be in direct competition with one another but they also assist one or the other in some ways since hardly any one among them is so completely independent and self-sufficient in everything they need. Like a rich men's club, they scratch one another's backs every now and then, exchanging favors that in the end bring about mutual or reciprocal benefits.

The poor, so-called Third World, or underdeveloped countries are the losers in this setup. They are kept on the outside looking in.

Their resources and cheap labor are exploited, always as peasants to the powerful landlords. Either that or they are always the customers who have to patronize the produce of the developed and technologically advanced nations, forced to buy at steep prices, whether or not they have something to sell themselves, and, if they do, at very little profit because of tariffs and/or various restrictions.

The leaders of the free world, which happen to also be from the richest and industrialized nations, keep on preaching, and enforcing where possible, the blessings of democracy and individual freedom of peoples all over the world.

Democracy and individual freedom are noble ideals – but they can be hindrances, indeed chains, for struggling countries and peoples.

How's that again? Democracy and individual freedom are chains for struggling countries and peoples?

Yes. Democracy and individual freedom and rights make it difficult, sometimes impossible, for a nation and its people to move resolutely in one direction to accomplish what is necessary for their advancement and progress.

The only way a country deficient in technology and capital resources can turn their fortunes around and make a leap toward progress and prosperity is by harnessing all available resources and its people's efforts to bring about maximized productivity and reduced dependence on foreign goods. This may sound simple and a no-brainer for all countries and peoples desiring a better collective and individual condition, but that is not so.

Different sectors and factions may have different opinions on how to go about accomplishing the national purpose. There may also be various self-interest groups, particularly industries, that want to maneuver for their best advantage. Citizens may not follow policies and regulations that run counter to their individual desires and tastes, like having to purchase local goods that are inferior in quality to imported ones, or doing without certain luxuries and pleasures. Some groups may actually try to overturn such policies, like those in the business of importation.

Strong leadership and governments, even authoritarian ones, are the only solutions to such situations. Often, if not always, individual freedom and choices have to be curtailed or restricted to achieve the larger purpose.

In the last century and through the start of the present, the countries that managed to rise from a lowly state to join the ranks of economically strong nations are those whose governments had little or no opposition that could block or slow down development programs and whose people either did not have the right to protest and object or were by culture subservient to their leaders.

Most of those countries are in Asia. Japan, Taiwan, Singapore, South Korea and China are the countries that moved up in economic and industrial status to be at par with, or at least respectably positioned in relation to, the established rich western giants like the US, Britain, Germany and France.

All these Asian countries did not develop their economies and industrial capabilities while governed under American or even European style democracy. Rather, they had either authoritarian or single-party governments or had very dominant parties holding power for prolonged periods of time; or had people who generally followed their leaders' policies and programs with no substantial opposition or recalcitrant sector.

For decades now, the US, UK, France and other industrialized nations have been advocating for democracy, free market and free trade, often making these conditions prerequisites to granting aid or opening their domestic markets to other countries. All these systems are beneficial mostly to the developed economies but often harmful to the poor countries, many of which will be better helped by strong, even authoritarian, governments and varying degrees of protectionism for their industries.

The World Trade Organization, with members accounting for 95 percent of the world's trade, will probably have to struggle for many, many years more to bring about an equitable sharing of economic benefits for all, or at least the majority, of its members.

THE ROAD TO UTOPIA

Achieving the perfect world, or at least getting close to universal contentment, or even just a nearly equal apportionment of material goods and opportunities for finding happiness, had seemed entirely impossible throughout history. It may ever be so but we now have a considerable chance of attaining those goals, if not one hundred percent then quite respectably near that degree.

Many will disagree with the propositions and theories that will be presented in this book. Some may agree with some of the ideas but find flaws and possibilities for failure of the other ideas.

No doubt, many intelligent minds, far superior in wisdom and expertise to this author, can propose better solutions. That is not cause for shame or disappointment to him; in fact, that is his wish. For "perfecting Utopia" cannot be achieved by one man's ideas alone, no man could be so gifted and omniscient; nor could it be done by the joining of a few brilliant minds. Rather, it can only be crafted by contributions from as many minds as can propose refinements to the basic propositions or even submit completely different approaches to the world's problems.

If anything, this author will be happy and consider his purposes fulfilled if what he has written here will trigger discussions and debates; or even just cause those superior minds to think that perhaps a much better world is possible and it is not that difficult to achieve, if only we recognize the obstacles to bringing about that better world in their true light, not necessarily as presented in this work - for the author may be grossly deficient in expertise and his analyses may be erroneous, and his capability to accomplish the task he so ambitiously tackled so pitifully inadequate.

It is entirely possible, even probable, that there are some aspects to the conditions of the world and modern man that were missed or not properly evaluated in this work. But, again, if this work sparks the interest of those who are more qualified and capable to take on the problems besetting human society worldwide, then the author has been richly rewarded for his humble, and perhaps ignorant, efforts.

What makes it seem, at least to this author, that we have a chance to attain a better life for everybody, or almost everybody, on this planet?

There appears to be a confluence of conditions in the present time that make it possible, and even necessary, to work out solutions to the greatest problems of mankind that would lead to that better, if not truly perfect, world.

First, the vast developments in science and technology of the past few decades have made possible the solutions to many problems.

Second, the emergence of problems of global proportions – like global warming, pollution, worldwide deforestation, extinction or near-extinction of countless species of flora and fauna (many of which may be vital to human existence as well as to the planet's viability as a cradle of life), imbalances and dangers to the environment, and, yes, even the global economic crisis of the first decade of the third millennium – are bringing together many, almost all, nations to seek avenues of cooperation and united courses of action.

Sooner or later, the most powerful nations in the world will have to forget or work out their differences and reconcile their divergent interests to overcome the greatest problems.

Soon afterward, as the powerful nations realize that they also need the cooperation of the weaker and poorer ones to bring about the results they intended, they will recognize that they must address the situations afflicting the latter to get them to join in the act.

Also, all nations will eventually recognize, as indeed many and even most of them have already done, that there are enormous benefits to be derived from joining forces. The European Union has proven that and there are so many non-member states waiting in line to join up. That despite the fact that the EU set up stringent requirements for membership and it has been imposing discipline on members who violate their laws and regulations.

NAFTA is limited to the three North American nations of Canada, the US and Mexico but they have also become APEC members, obviously realizing that APEC is the sleeping giant, with so many members comprising the bulk of the world's population.

APEC is not anywhere near achieving the true solidarity of the EU which has not only opened their borders to member countries but share a single monetary unit, the euro; but the fact that it was organized is proof most countries are aware of the need to adapt to the present era of geopolitics and macro-economics and to eventually traverse the path blazed by the EU.

No region in the world has as much diversity in race and culture as Asia and the Pacific. Unlike Europe where all native peoples are Caucasian, and Africa where people are mostly of Negroid stock, on the Asian mainland alone there are Caucasians, Malays, Aryan, Mongolian, and Chinese, who are physically so different from one another. On the island chains to the south and to the Pacific, there are Japanese, aborigines, pygmies and Polynesians. All these peoples have cultures and ways of life as diverse as their physical characteristics.

These differences, along with economic disparities and competition, may be hindering the coming together of Asiatic peoples but the presence of Americans and Canadians, who joined APEC as it is in their best interests to do so, may help them discard narrow parochial interests and biases and adopt an ecumenical and cosmopolitan viewpoint.

If China and Japan can set aside generations-old animosities to work together for the welfare of their coming generations, with the US as steadying influence, APEC can be one cohesive unit that may well be the biggest player in world trade.

A WORLD GOVERNMENT: THE ONLY WAY

If and when APEC becomes as strong as, or stronger than, the EU then it will become apparent to both that it will be better for them to join forces and cooperate instead of working at cross purposes. Trade wars, after all, can be just as devastating as the military kind when they cause economies to crash and wipe out industries and people's livelihoods.

They will thereafter realize that having the rest of the world to get into the act will be even better as it will lead to maximizing and harmonizing the productivity and economic activities of all nations and peoples, as well as stabilizing all the regions for the continuing benefit of each and everyone.

The need for a lasting peace and diligent cooperation of all countries can only be possible with a supreme authority overseeing all the world's affairs. Thus, the stage will be set for a world government.

That world government, besides establishing peace and economic order, will also be the key to solving the planet's most critical problems. It is, in fact, the world's, and mankind's, only hope.

Otherwise, how can we contain pollution of the earth's atmosphere and the deterioration of the ozone layer? How can we prevent the denudation of the world's green cover?

Too, how else can we put an end to wars, big and small, genocide and religious strife, or tyrannical governments?

There is also that very vital and all-encompassing factor of the world economy, which, as we painfully realized to the fullest in the early part of the third millennium, affects all nations and individuals, regardless of station. Competing financial institutions, industries and multinational commercial conglomerates cannot be allowed to operate without an international comptroller.

And then there is the matter of providing for the needs of the very poor nations and the very destitute people, specially those suffering from famine, lack of viable natural resources and technological capabilities.

Simply, how else can we save people and the world itself?

The US and the other rich nations contribute the greatest volume of toxic elements to the planet's air and waters. They advocate pollution reduction and concern for the environment but do not themselves practice what they preach because it would mean reducing industrial production and sacrificing their prosperity.

The poor tropical countries lack viable sources of income and their rich jungles provide them with a large part of their revenue through logs and timber products. They seem to have little or no awareness that the earth's vegetation, wherever it exists, is part and parcel of the planet's lifeline.

Those that have exotic fauna put them on the pet market, or butcher them for food like stock animals, unmindful of the fact that those creatures may be vital strands in the web of life and are all living treasures that belong not only to humanity but Mother Nature and, thus, planet Earth – nay, the universe - or, shall we say for want of a better word, creation.

For better or worse, what each country does in its own territory affects the entire planet. Yet, how will France stop Indonesia from cutting its trees or how can the US prevent Colombians from razing jungles to plant coca to make cocaine, or how can Australia stop poachers in Kenya from killing elephants for the ivory trade and Indians from hunting tigers for their skins and rhino for their horns?

We cannot go on forever this way. Fact is, we cannot go on much longer this way. Soon or late, but it has to be soon, nations big and small must band, bind and bond together, as a matter of mutual and collective survival.

The poor tropical nations, however, cannot be forced to cease exploiting their forests and other natural resources unless they are provided with alternative sources of revenue, or are given direct material aid in return for conserving such.

But even if the wealthy nations were willing to undertake such measures, the desired results cannot be ensured without a strong international organization to oversee all aspects and procedures entailed in the universal effort to save the planet.

Some countries may fear that the powerful nations, particularly the United States, will dominate a world government. But the European Union has found a way to govern itself in a democratic and egalitarian system. It will not be impossible, nor too difficult, to formulate a similar setup for a world government.

Also, it must be remembered that the world government, whichever country or whoever are at the helm, will have to provide for the needs and welfare of everybody, otherwise the said government will fail and the nations and peoples will break up into various factions of divergent interests and situations and chaos would ensue. So it really does not matter who shall be at the top at any given time, the duties and functions will be well-delineated and inviolable.

The world government, before it can seriously and effectively address the material needs of all the countries and peoples of the planet, must first have to stop the conflicts between nations, cultures and religions for there can be no true worldwide cooperation unless universal peace, stability and order are established.

The Middle East will be the most difficult region to pacify and stabilize but with a world government resolutely pursuing these objectives, with no parties outside of those concerned taking a stance different from said government, the matter will be more manageable. There will no longer be separate hidden agendas for the US, Russia, China, Britain, Germany. The world government's objective will be the only and final consideration.

Besides the threat of economic, industrial and technological isolation, the possibility of military action against those that violate or do not conform to the policies of the world government will be very decisive. For the world government will be able to act with greater firmness and dispatch than the

United Nations or NATO was ever capable of, since it will no longer have to depend on token forces under separate commands of participating nations which have their individual political concerns to consider.

The Israelis and the Arabs will also have one very strong reason to make peace and for good. They no longer have to fear each other since the world government can assure the security of all parties and the enforcement of provisions of all agreements they shall enter into.

In other areas where there is armed violence, civil war or border disputes, like in some countries in Africa and Asia, order can be established either through mediation by international peace counselors or, when stronger measures are called for, adequate peacekeeping forces.

Where the causes of conflict are age-old tribal hatreds, the knowledge that neither will be allowed to continue harassing the other, much less decimate their enemies, with Big Brother ready to swing the big stick, will force those violent pseudo-chiefs to the negotiating table or back home to their villages.

The main reason there are so many pockets of unwieldy armed power in Africa is the lack of strong organized civil authority that can subjugate the warlords. The poverty and human suffering brought about by this lack of proper government must and will be addressed by the operation of strong local and regional leaderships fully supported with finances, logistics and military force, if necessary, by the world government.

Once stability is brought into these areas, then the problems of food supply, poverty and lack of opportunity can be addressed.

It must be emphasized that besides looking after the welfare of nations and peoples the world government will also have to provide for the fulfillment of the needs and desires of the individual person; for discontented individuals, when strongly aroused or motivated, can create problems for the greater body of society, most especially when many individuals of similar circumstances organize themselves to force others to listen and address their needs or desires.

There may be a delicate problem concerning the Muslims and Arabs, as well as other religious-cultural groups whose way of life and beliefs are different from the secular and rationalist practices and attitudes that will surely prevail in the happy world we are striving for.

Some of them will prefer to remain closed societies maintaining their customs and laws based on their ancient history and heritage. That, of course, is a choice that is perfectly within their rights. They may prefer not to join a world government that may have policies and programs that intrude or violate their own religious beliefs and traditions.

However, there are Arab and Muslim leaders and states that have been moving toward liberalism and secularization or at least some degree of tolerance of previously taboo practices within their societies. As this is being written, many of them have been undergoing political upheavals which may also bring about cultural and attitudinal changes. The time may not be far off when the obstinately conservative enclaves will be isolated not only from the non-Muslim world but also among fellow Islamic states.

But those that elect to retain their conservative culture should be allowed to do so, provided that their traditions and practices do not prejudice other states, societies and peoples. The realities of modern existence, however, will inevitably convince them that they have to join the rest of the world, since they will surely need goods, services and technological assistance and cooperation with countries and regions outside their limited boundaries and spheres.

Where they control areas or resources that are vital to other sectors of the world, as in oil or transport routes, they can be made to appreciate the importance of either joining the international community in some degree of assimilation or accommodation or making compromise agreements.

In such a situation, the promise of continuous supply of goods or whatever they need and the counterbalance of the possibility of withholding them in some form of embargo may be very powerful factors. It is also possible that some or all of the Islamic states may band together as a bloc to join or transact with the world government as a single, unified entity.

As to the other isolationist communities, they are mostly minuscule undeveloped pockets in regions where they can be bypassed or easily persuaded to make mutually beneficial pacts with the international community.

Unless a country or region is self-sufficient in everything it needs, it will have to interact with others in different parts of the globe, and it has to join the world government for the sake of survival.

Alas, but then perhaps fortunately, no country or people can afford to be insular now. No isolationist and cloistered societies could survive with any degree of normalcy and comfort.

It will also be petty and antisocial to attempt to perpetuate the purity of races, cultures and ways of life, and thus try to separate ourselves from others. The world has become global, and our attitudes must adapt to the new realities, or, shall we say, eternal truths that we failed to see before in our myopic self-centeredness.

We must break down the ancient barriers that have prevented us from joining up with one another, the divisions forged by nations and religions, as well, indeed, as differences in races and cultures. These modes of identity used to be causes of pride and distinction. However, they also pulled us apart and suppressed our true and common identity.

The most recent studies of the human genome reveal that all people on earth, wherever they come from, no matter their physical characteristics, are descended from a single male and a single female ancestor - Adam and Eve, in the scientific sense - who originated in Africa.

They were not the only humans to have lived in the dawn of time; they did not even happen to live at the same time, but theirs are the only genes that survived in all modern humans. They are the roots of that single family tree to which we all trace our individual origins.

Yes, we are one family. Despite geographic distances and variations in appearance we are of the same inherent nature.

We may call them by different names, but we have similar basic dreams and aspirations, as well as identical emotions and feelings – the same causes for sorrow as well as for joy.

Is not the laughter and sparkle in the eye of a young Spanish señorita just as sweet and heartwarming as that of a teenage girl in Hongkong?

Conversely, is the anguish of a destitute African-American woman with a sick child in Harlem any more, or any less, than that of the Indian mother in Mumbai?

Socrates said, "I am not Athenian, neither am I Greek. I am a citizen of the world."

You are not French. She is not Buddhist. I am not whatever.

You are a human being. So is she. As I am. That is all we are. That is all that matters.

A brotherhood of man.

"Imagine all the people living life in peace."

CASHLESS ECONOMY: THE END OF FINANCIAL CRIMES

Once the world government has been established, there are a number of systems that have to be institutionalized worldwide to facilitate the effective administration of all human affairs.

Obviously, a universal unit of currency is a must. This will rationalize all international as well as local commerce and economic matters.

There is another system that must be implemented for the utmost efficiency and security of all financial transactions and interaction: a cashless monetary structure.

In this age of automated banking, it will be quite easy, and eventually necessary, for people to do away with cash or portable money. Besides being inconvenient, physically taking currency on one's person also requires many consequential actions connected with the use and disbursement of cash – like bringing a wallet or billfold, counting bills, producing exact change, etc. In place of all that, one may only have to bring a card, swipe it and punch numbers on a keyboard. Eventually, he may not need a card at all. Using fingerprints or photographs of a person's iris to identify the account owner may become both a safeguard as well as a convenient substitute for an ATM card.

Yes, automated banking is the key. It will be ideal if every human being is provided with his or her own financial account from childhood, or at whatever age it will be deemed legal for a person to enter into financial transactions, and all the person's monetary dealings all his or her life shall be processed through that account.

This setup will solve many of the problems involving money that have beset people, institutions and governments since man found it necessary to establish a medium of exchange to replace direct barter of goods in doing trade and commerce.

First, a person could no longer lose his money because he misplaced or forgot it somewhere. Not only that, it could no longer be stolen. Too, if a person is defrauded or coerced by another into transferring money, under whatever circumstances, into another's account, it will be easy to prove that such an event occurred as the bank – or whatever financial institution is established to oversee the world's monetary transactions – shall have a record of the transfer.

Extortion, blackmail and bribery will therefore be very risky, and presumably will be greatly reduced or even nearly eradicated from human dealings. And that is only on the individual level.

Bank robberies, hijackings, corporate fraud and most other crimes involving property will be a thing of the past.

Taxes, if some form of it has to be collected from certain transactions, will be easy to determine and deducted as all transactions will be on record. It may even be possible to collect taxes simultaneously with the transaction, simplifying this hitherto messy and complicated procedure which is also fraught with fraudulent practices.

If no cash exists, nothing can change hands clandestinely but material goods, that will be mostly visible and could not have high value – except for items like gold and precious stones.

This is where the proposition that gold and gems that command prices disproportionate to their utilitarian worth be devalued and priced according to their true service to people's needs, becomes vital and indispensable.

It may be argued that the value people put on things and their desirability cannot be dictated or philosophized upon. But look what dedicated campaigns and information drives accomplished against wearing furs and alligator shoes, bags, and other such things that used to feed the vanity of those who could afford them.

The public outcry against this cruelty to animals caused most commerce on these items to stop. The fur and reptile skin trades have since resumed but with strict regulations such that the animals they are derived from are bred, raised and cared for with the greatest attention for their well-being and the manner of slaughter made quick, less painful and stressful. Also, the fact that the animals are already farm-bred and - raised and no longer so rare has brought down prices and, consequently, status value and demand.

Without physical currency that can actually change hands and with monetary values of metals and stones that are precious at present brought down, it will be almost impossible to profit from most material and property crimes.

In many instances, extortion and bribery could only be in the form of sexual favors or the like, which could not be very profitable to the extortionist or bribe-taker and could only be occasional.

And then, too, the fact that the sectors of the world that are members of the unified government do not use cash and operate under a computerized credit system will totally preclude transactions with non-members except under some sort of barter system. This, however, will be highly inconvenient and unwieldy in most situations; particularly when the material to be bartered is voluminous or perishable or for some other reason difficult to transport quickly and the physical distance between the parties engaging in the transaction is great.

Abolition of physical currency therefore will be another compelling reason for all countries to join the unified world government as only by being part of its cashless financial structure can all individuals and entities transact with the larger world.

LEADERS FAITHFUL AND TRUE

The people who will run the world government will naturally be competent and conscientious in the performance of their duties as they will be nominated by their home countries and could be presumed to be highly qualified and reliable. They will be incapable of abuse since so many people and organizations will be monitoring their actions and most of their decisions will be according to a stringent set of rules. Further, their tenure will be short and temporary.

It is in the aspect of national and local governments that abuse of power may still occur. Even if the world government can be imbued with supervisory and oversight powers, it may have a hard time keeping track of every country, region and community and passing judgment on all political conflicts as well as legal, social and humanitarian issues.

Governments should ideally be led by people who only have service to the people or the community at heart, over and above their personal pecuniary needs and interests. Alas, the ideal could not be attained with certainty or even considerable frequency and the honest and conscientious leader has appeared as a rarity throughout history. Humanity has had very few Nelson Mandelas.

But there is a way we can have ONLY true and dedicated statesmen lead governments all over the planet.

This can be done by making top government posts non-paying but permanent and hereditary. Yes, leaders will be like monarchs whose offspring – either the eldest or most capable, preferably the latter – shall take over upon their death, disability or retirement.

If a leader's son or daughter is already ordained to succeed him, then that son or daughter can be trained from the earliest years for the job that awaits him or her. There will be no incompetent high officials. The heir apparent can even be given on the job training and assist the parent perform some of the tasks of governance.

A leader who knows his offspring and grandchildren, and so on, will inherit his position shall exert all effort to bring about the best situation in the territory or community that his bloodline shall inherit like a kingdom, so long as they fulfill their role with competence and fidelity. Yes, there must be a standard of job performance for it to be retained by the leader and his progeny.

Oh, and there is the small matter of compensation.

The top leaders of government shall not be compensated financially for their lifetime of work. Aside from that, they, and their immediate family, shall be disqualified from owning property and their financial accounts frozen or deactivated for so long as a member of the family holds the position.

All their needs, however, will be provided for along a standard befitting their status. In other words, every member of the immediate family will be enjoying a life of comfort and dignity with no need to worry about their material requirements so long as the family retains the post, so that each member has a motivation to help in the proper dispensation of the official duties.

Should one of the official's family commit an abuse, the rest of the family will surely rebuke and strive to keep the offending member in line as their collective and individual futures are being endangered. Should the family lose the office then the members would have to fend for themselves in the outside world for which, if they had been in the office for many years, they may be lacking in preparation and training.

It may be posited that few individuals will be interested in being government officials under such conditions and those that may be interested and willing may find their spouses and children opposed to the idea. But there are many such people in the world – they are just not usually in government or politics. Yes, such people, by the very nature of their sterling character, do not desire, much less seek, power.

For instance, even among the wealthiest people are some very pro-poor souls, including certain ones that devote their lives to helping and serving others, often having to endure and share the squalor and miserable conditions of their beneficiaries, totally forsaking the comfort and luxury that they should have been enjoying.

Look at the volunteers for Greenpeace, some of them well-educated professionals who not only forgo lucrative careers but even risk life and limb to protect nature and the environment. Look at the missionaries and charity workers in Africa's poorest countries.

Think of Dian Fosey and Jane Goodall, who devoted their lives (Fosey even lost hers) to protect the mountain gorilla and the chimpanzee while living in the African jungles. Think of Mahatma Gandhi. Best of all, think of Mother Teresa.

There ARE and HAVE BEEN people who want to serve and have served the world and humanity without any material compensation. In many cases, they serve selflessly even without the simple reward of recognition of their sacrifices.

Yes, Virginia, there are heroes among us.

MINIMIZING CRIME AND IMMORALITY

Crime and immorality, like armed conflict and organized violence, have to be eliminated or reduced to the barest minimum for society, specially a worldwide one, to function and thrive with the greatest sense of security and well-being for its members.

Aside from outright prevention through various means, the greatest deterrent to the commission of crime and practice of immoral acts, as was mentioned in a previous chapter, is the certainty, or strong probability, that the perpetrator will be found out, identified and brought to justice.

The criminals that are most difficult to apprehend are those with no previous record of offenses. They are farthest from suspicion and no past behavior would give clues pointing in their direction. Because of that, they will also be the ones most difficult to prevent from committing crimes a second or third time.

Science is moving fast towards discovering the true and deep-rooted causes of criminal behavior and finding ways to solve this most insidious and ancient sociological problem.

Advances in genetic engineering will, in the not-so-distant future, make it possible to identify which genes are connected to, and responsible for, criminal and other impulses – just as disease-related genes are being pinpointed and catalogued.

In the same way that diseases may soon be cured by genetic procedures, it will not be long before people with criminal and other harmful behavioral tendencies can be identified and treated genetically to cure them of those tendencies and thus preclude them as potential menaces to society.

But since we cannot hope for immediate efficacious scientific remedies to criminal tendencies, we can only hope to prevent or minimize their manifestations in the best ways within our present capabilities or what will be doable in the near future.

Foremost among the technologies being used in developed countries to check on persons with criminal backgrounds is the GPS (Global Positioning System) tracking device. With this attached to a known offender, said person will be unable to hide, and his or her presence at the scene of a crime can be proven.

Since the device makes it impossible to physically escape and escape accountability, it is a most effective prevention measure.

But the most efficient way to use GPS for crime prevention and prosecution is to place it on every living person - not just known criminals. A universal GPS for everybody will allow investigators to identify all persons who had been at a crime scene at the incriminating time and facilitate quicker resolutions to every violation of society's laws that are perpetrated with the physical presence or proximity of the culprit.

That is the system that could make bringing criminals to justice a very strong probability, indeed, almost a certainty.

Then, too, the placing of tracking devices on everybody has tremendous benefits beyond preventing and solving crimes. GPS tracking on ordinary people will ensure that no one goes or remains missing due to accidents, mishaps or loss of orientation, or even foul play and violent acts.

Parents and other family members will have peace of mind because they will be assured of being able to find their loved ones at all times. This will be most important when it involves those that are very young or with physical handicaps or dangerous ailments like heart disease, epilepsy or Alzheimer's condition, people who are most at risk when moving outside their homes.

Ah, but there will surely arise controversies and protests against tracking devices from different sectors, most of them centering on the invasion of privacy. This may seem a valid issue at first blush, but, really, what harm will disclosure of one's whereabouts at a given time do to him?

Will his visit to some museum or whole day's stint at the office, or an hour meandering through a supermarket, be something that ought to be kept from somebody else's knowledge? In an age when practically everyone has a personal mobile phone a person in such locations should be easily reachable. When he or she could not be contacted, then there should be cause for some concern.

It is possible that the person that cannot be reached has met an accident or is in some sort of predicament, suffered a heart attack or had been the victim of physical assault. It is in the personal interest of most people that they can be located when they cannot be contacted or are unable to communicate with others, most specially their family or friends.

It is mainly those who engage in nefarious and criminal activities who have reason to refuse and shun tracking devices, and they will be a minuscule minority, albeit a very vociferous and vicious one.

Criminal groups, terrorists and their minions and agents will be at the forefront of opposition to the system. They will be supported, purportedly in the name of decency and respect for individual rights, by philandering husbands and even wives who have secret affairs or vices that they want to keep secret.

There will be few legitimate concerns against universal GPS tracking and they will surely be outweighed by the vastly greater number of people who will be benefited by it, along with government, business and, most of all, society as a whole.

Further, to give everyone some measure of privacy in his or her activities, the matter of tracking someone through the GPS can be limited to certain situations and upon the instigation of a select few who have legitimate reasons to be concerned or interested in a particular individual's whereabouts and circumstances.

For added protection of privacy, a policy can be instituted, for instance, whereby only authorized personnel of the tracking agency will communicate with the object individual once he or she is traced and said individual will then be directly asked if he or she wishes to communicate with the party that is searching for him or her, or if he or she wishes to reveal his or her whereabouts, or whatever information he or she wishes relayed to the other party to allay fears regarding his or her extant circumstances.

If, however, the "searchee" or "trackee" cannot be reached by his mobile phone and could not be summoned through a public address system (if he is in a public place like a shopping mall or an office building) then it is possible he is in a predicament and the greatest value of the universal GPS coverage will come into operation. The local authorities of the area he has been traced to will be alerted to check on him where he was traced through GPS. He may be needing immediate medical attention or police assistance or even rescue.

Such incidents and instances, basing from our experiences, will not be very rare.

As regards immorality, GPS tracking will surely have an effect on infidelity as well as activities that have to be indulged in at certain specific places, like gambling, bar drinking, engaging prostitutes, etc. But there definitely will be ways for those who are really hooked on to certain vices or pastimes to do their thing and keep these affairs secret.

It will be ideal, of course, if we can curtail such activities through education and moral campaigns or even stringent laws. However, where the "immoral" acts do no harm to other individuals, perhaps injuring only those who engage in them, a consequence they consciously accept in exchange for the pleasure they derive from their acts, then we can allow them the "privacy" of the individual.

PROVIDING FOR
EVERYONE'S NEEDS

This is obviously the most difficult problem to overcome. It will require the greatest universal effort as well as the longest period of experimentation, trial-and-error fits and starts, and steadfast collective determination and utmost flexibility.

What will be presented here are not necessarily THE solutions or parts of THE solutions. For all will be just ideas, meant only to illustrate that the objective can be attained, at least in theory, because of the convergence of advances in technology, the state of international relations and cooperation, and the evolution of global economics, environmental conditions and problems affecting not a few countries or regions but the whole planet.

With a unified government - the lynchpin of our Utopia - in place, qualified and honest officials running both the world as well as most local and regional governments; a cashless financial system already established, and a crime prevention and criminal prosecution network operating with the most advanced technologies – the world can buckle down to the monumental task of providing the needs of every human.

The first step is to undertake studies to identify the economic hotspots that most need large-scale assistance programs and seek to dovetail those programs with other problems in other countries.

What this means is that economy of effort as well as expense should be strived for to optimize the use of all resources. There are situations where solving certain problems - instead of creating other, sometimes greater, problems as happens in many cases - can actually provide solutions to other, sometimes even greater, predicaments. These possibilities, of course, would come about only because there is a world government that can orchestrate all international and local activities

The most constant and never-ending need to be met is food production. Clothing can be used over and over, shelter is permanent or usable for a long time. But food is consumed day in, day out.

There have been amazing breakthroughs in the field of food production and many countries have a surplus in crops. Yet, masses of people starve in many regions of Africa and food aid sent to them do not always reach the intended beneficiaries due to peace and order problems, with many warlords in armed conflict. Even if the problem of warlords and other hindrances to food distribution are overcome, the cost of transporting hundreds or even thousands of tons of food supplies is staggering.

Instead of sending food and other things to the destitute and undeveloped regions, a better way is to export the technology that allows other countries to produce more than their own needs to these regions. Modern agriculture and manufacturing techniques can be introduced, along with appropriate education and training, to countries lagging in productivity.

With the advent of modern methods of farming like hydroponics, aquaponics and aeroponics, as well as vertical agriculture, crops can be grown and even fish, poultry and small livestock can be raised where there is no real farmland or fisheries, and often more economically and efficiently.

Technology has developed such that plants can be made independent of the need for direct sunlight, which could be very unreliable on cloudy days or during rainy or cold seasons. Reciprocally, in the present methods of modern agriculture, no one has to pray for rain, nor even resort to scientifically-induced precipitation to irrigate farmlands.

Plants, fish and many farm animals thrive in conditions managed to the optimum such as are not possible or easily achievable on a constant basis in traditional or natural methods.

Crops can grow even in barren desert when the medium is nutrient-fed water, not soil. Where there is little open space available, rooftops can be planted to vegetables, pens of small livestock can be maintained in multi-tiered structures. The space required is much less yet the yields are even far greater as the processes are more dynamically controlled.

With proper adaptation of technology to almost any living conditions and any terrain, people can produce their own food practically anywhere.

The need for vast tracts of surface land for farms will be greatly reduced, or even dispensed with. So will the need to transport the produce across great distances to reach markets and consumers.

Thus, we will be releasing and reverting more and more of the land we cultivated for crops to nature, to becoming savannahs, prairies, wilderness. Perhaps some of those former farmlands can be transformed into forests and jungles again. And then some, perhaps many, of the wildlife we have pushed to marginal survival through devastation of their habitat can thrive once more.

To more efficiently distribute food and other necessities to the world's people, it is essential that we make them more accessible – the people, that is, to infrastructure, public services and almost all things that need to be provided them. In most instances, it will be more economical and practical, as well as less destructive to the environment, to bring people to where infrastructure already exists or where more people will be served by such - instead of building infrastructure wherever people are situated.

If the inhabitants of far-flung villages can be brought together to form communities around farming and industrial centers, they can provide the work force and also be the clientele of the commercial establishments that are extant or will consequently blossom within the peripheries of those centers.

If most, preferably all, people can be gathered in urban areas, to towns where they can join the larger communities, then everyone can more easily be benefited by all the blessings of modern civilization and technology.

The children can go to schools, the health concerns of everyone can be monitored and attended to, job opportunities identified and allocated. It will be easier to manage larger populations.

From such urbanized areas, people can have specific and specialized training for jobs in countries where there is a need for more workers. This will ease the "brain drain" in developing nations whose top professionals are being siphoned off by the richer countries, thus stunting or slowing down the growth and development of their homelands.

Another benefit to be derived from collecting and gathering of people into population and production hubs is environmental - in an aspect entirely separate from the avoidance of infrastructure construction. The damage and pressure on the ecology caused by people in hinterlands and far-flung coasts trying to wrestle out a living and survive in harsh conditions will be largely eliminated.

There may be a special and diverse set of approaches to be employed towards indigenous peoples. Some of them can and must be assimilated into the general culture of their region and eventually adapt to the way of life in urbanized areas.

There will surely be howls from certain quarters about preserving the cultures and way of life of the likes of natives of South American jungles and Papua New Guinea. But are not the old ways of these indigenous peoples being diluted and altered by exposure to modern humans? And are not many of them dying out in many hidden jungle habitats, some have vanished entirely - the very reason for their rarity?

We could not, should not, doom them to remaining in their primitive state, forever battling with the harshness of uncivilized existence, just so we can gawk at them like they were zoo animals and watch videos of them on National Geographic and Discovery Channel. They are human beings, not a platypus or a coelacanth. One of them may turn out to be an Einstein or a Shakespeare.

If a brother or a sister who got lost and separated from our family as a child was found later surviving like an animal or a prehistoric human in some forest, would we be willing to leave him or her in that sad state? To eventually perish to nothingness, forgotten and forsaken like an obscure, inconsequential leaf that fell from an unidentified tree to rot on the ground?

Sure, some of them may refuse and resist being yanked out from their wilderness home and be transported to a whole new world – that is but natural of most everybody who will be taken to unfamiliar, strange and possibly fearsome surroundings. But social workers and psychologists and other experts can exert determined efforts to convince them that such a move will give them a better life and a better future.

If psychological and cultural shackles could not be overcome then perhaps a more subtle, slower process can be devised to eventually persuade them to join the rest of humanity for their own good.

Or perhaps, to facilitate enforcing of the program to assimilate all people into the larger community, laws may be enacted to declare the habitats the primitive people obstinately cling to as nature sanctuaries or preserves where humans are prohibited from trespassing or residing. Thus, legal procedures and actions may be taken to achieve the purpose. This may seem cruel, but there will always be situations when, as the saying goes, "one cannot make an omelet without breaking eggs."

But there are, of course, among the indigenous people those who are thriving in their natural and native habitat and also some who may be in grave danger if made to live elsewhere, particularly where they may be exposed to diseases, microorganisms and toxic elements that their physiological nature has no defenses for.

These people will be best left to continue their existence in their ancestral environments. Perhaps some agency can be established to monitor their conditions for their own welfare and protection.

Once the physical locations and transfigurations of population compositions are largely managed and controlled for efficient distribution of goods and services and maximized productivity of each population group, the formulation of the systems and programs to provide for the needs of the world's people in the most equitable manner can begin.

It should be stressed that poor people will not be welfare or charity wards of society. Their being gathered together in population centers where most institutions of productivity, education and job training can be found or established is for the purpose of determining fields they can fill niches in.

Those still too young or undergoing training or education will be provided all their needs until they can earn their keep. Those too old or weak can still find ways to be useful, or at least be placed in homes where they can be cared for by experts in the most unintrusive and cost-saving manner such that they are not too much of a burden to society as well as their personal families who will be free to perform their tasks and daily activities instead of having to tend to their elderly or physically incapable kin.

There will be enormous costs in feeding, clothing and housing the multitudes of humanity but most of them will be pulling their own weight. In the course of several years - certainly within a generation - most people of working age and physical condition will be functioning to his or her own and the community's benefit.

Since keeping most of the people in organized communities facilitates the easy identification of their skills and abilities and placing them where they can be productive, the economy will operate more efficiently. If there is a surfeit of certain skills then the less proficient can be retrained in other endeavors.

Some of those who came from forest or jungle habitats can be allowed to stay at or near their familiar surroundings to oversee the rejuvenation of the environment and report or directly tackle ecological problems that may arise. Or they can guide and assist scientists and researchers mapping out the vast variety of life and the structures of nature or seeking new sources of medicine.

Farming people without education or training in other fields can be assigned to macro farms, which, though possibly different from their own plots, will still be the sort of work they know best and where they can be useful with some retraining and introduction to modern methods of agriculture.

Because all people are provided for while they are not gainfully employed they will not be pressed to find work just to survive. Unlike the present day when everybody, except for the affluent, has to make a living, even in demeaning and miserable conditions, those without jobs can find trades most suitable to their knowhow and talents, or seek out employers offering the best compensation – or otherwise reinvent themselves so they can gain new and better-paid skills.

Employers, on the other hand, may not be able to exploit cheap, desperate labor but the workers they eventually hire will be more proficient and dedicated since those workers will be performing work they themselves have chosen and acquired mastery in.

Of course, there is the problem of the lowest-ranked, low-paying menial jobs which normally gets filled by the unskilled and poorest individuals who may no longer wish to take them on since they are being provided their basic needs even without working.

Here, some system of forcible or mandatory delegation of work to those who are beneficiaries of social subsidy may have to be instituted. Those who are able-bodied and unemployed, specially those with families also receiving allotments for basic needs, may be required to take on the jobs that no one wants.

Further, from the salaries of those who are subsidized a certain portion must be deducted to somehow repay government's expenditures for them. Or perhaps, if the family income is insufficient for their subsistence, then most, or even all, of the income will be turned over to the state or whatever agency is in charge of providing their needs so that they will not be a complete burden to society. When the workers are making enough money to sustain themselves and their families they will no longer be beneficiaries and will be classified as self-supporting.

With well-organized communities functioning not only as centers for living and production but also for training workers for various fields, the establishments and nations looking for work forces for their industries can embark on programs of recruitment and even direct training for their specific labor needs.

There may be those who will doubt whether the various national governments and peoples of affluent nations, who will naturally bear the greatest financial burden of providing for the needs of the destitute of the world, will acquiesce to such a sacrifice through a continuing duration until the latter gradually and individually become self-sustaining. There will be protests and objections from a number of sectors in those countries, even from the governments themselves, but eventually they will have to accede to the urgent necessity of such international financial transfusion.

The United States funnels hundreds of billions of dollars through prolonged periods to finance wars or prevent and protect itself against them. The United Kingdom, Japan and Germany contribute to international peacekeeping missions as well as food and medical assistance to the poor countries or those that suffered natural disasters. China spends so much to keep its military as modern as their available resources and technology will allow.

Sometimes nations deliberately hold down their production of food, oil and other goods just to keep prices at a certain level, and even go to the extent of actually destroying crops and produce so the market does not get flooded with surplus stocks.

Well, they can channel such funds and send surplus produce to Africa and East Timor and Bangladesh. Particularly with a world government rendering huge national military forces unnecessary and, presumably, overseeing the rational operation of economic forces, international cooperation and assistance may become higher in the ladder of priority of national appropriations.

Surely, the G-20 countries will be more than willing to allocate a considerable percentage of their government budgets to prevent subsistence farmers from continually destroying Indonesia's vast jungles for slash-and-burn planting; or destitute communities in India from clearing out forests to sell wood products and open up croplands.

They would also like blast fishing in Philippine waters to end so that coral reefs and other important parts of the underwater environment do not get decimated. Brazil has to be convinced, even perhaps compensated, to stop clearing vast tracts of pristine forest for conversion to soy bean plantations.

These things are no longer just local problems since the ecosystem is very vital to the entire world; what happens to Brazil's rainforests affect the glaciers in the North Pole and thence the sea level in Holland and the temperature in New York.

The loss of some seemingly insignificant species may snap the chain of the web of life that can spell disaster for other species, including those vital to man's existence and well-being.

There will be huge bills to pay, and the world has to fork out the wherewithal. It is the only way we can survive in the long run.

And, happily, it will also be the way to achieving the better world we all wish for.

REDRAWING BOUNDARIES

As the world government and the world's peoples bring about planetwide cooperation, there will be constant and mutually beneficial exchanges of people and resources and progressively expanding financial and economic activities.

Many developed nations will need infusions of people, mainly young workers, to replace and support their aging population.

The developed countries have longer, and continually lengthening, average lifespans and their citizens, consequently, are aging to the point of becoming truly aged. Since they are not producing enough offspring to replace those reaching retirement age, the proportion of the old to the young is progressively increasing.

The social security systems of many developed countries are experiencing the strain of growing numbers of retirees that have to be paid pensions for longer periods. When the system was first formulated, not very many people lived up to the retirement age of 65 years, and then, of those few retirees, fewer still lived beyond another five years or so.

Today so many workers reach retirement age and the retirees –due to improved medication and health care – are living longer, thus remaining on social security payrolls well beyond the projections that had gone into the program's computations and fiscal rationale.

With the sector of young, productive citizens shrinking in both number and in proportion to the retirees, fewer workers are making social security contributions that should help support pension funds.

The situation is reversed in the underdeveloped countries that are producing more and more young people while the lifespan of their citizens, though increasing due to advances in medicine and health care, is less than that in affluent nations.

Surely, there is a way to fit in these contrary conditions like reverse poles of a magnet. It may not be all that simple, but flexible minds can work out the intricacies and stumbling blocks, given that the situations at both ends do not submit to easy or even perceptible solutions by themselves and in their own spheres.

Many of the industrialized nations have been accepting immigrants to bolster their work force in fields where the indigenous workers lack expertise or refuse to be employed, such as in the lowly and menial labor sectors; or where the available local workers are not enough for the demand.

This may be a perfect setup for both host countries and migrant workers during times of economic and industrial stability but when conditions shift the natives sometimes find that they are crowded out by their guests, who normally receive less than the locals, and are, for that very reason, preferred by employers.

There are also many situations where the foreigners are better educated, more intelligent and diligent, for usually it is the best and the brightest that are given priority of entry and employment by host nations and establishments, hence the "brain drain".

When a host nation's own citizens are competing for jobs with migrant workers, specially when the latter are better-skilled or more diligent, the government, or the institution providing employment, will have to contend with political as well as practical issues.

If the employer favors the locals to comply with national policies or economic programs or out of patriotism, the better-skilled migrant workers will be lost to the employer, possibly forever as these may find jobs in other countries and never return even when conditions for their reemployment are better.

Meanwhile, the countries of origin of the migrant workers will not regain the talents they lost even if said workers left their erstwhile foreign employers, as the workers will most probably seek new employment in other foreign lands, having known and gotten used to the level of income attainable outside their motherland.

It may, however, be possible to provide the workers with the required skills and cerebral capacities without siphoning away the smart professionals from less-developed countries so that a "win-win" situation in the long haul can be achieved.

After all, if a rich industrialized nation should try to attract the professionals and skilled workers they need just through generous compensation packages, they may find other industrialized economies trying to outbid them for those workers. Thus, the workers they hire may suddenly leave them for better-paying employers elsewhere since material reward is the main, and presumably the only, reason for their relationship. Sometimes the workers are just using one host nation as a jumping board to other, more affluent, nations, or higher positions elsewhere, after gaining "international experience" to boost their qualifications.

On the other side of the coin, the workers may also be prone to feelings of insecurity since they may be displaced by natives who may develop skills equal to them, or by other foreign workers willing to accept less pay.

What will arise in either or both the aforementioned scenarios is a state of instability and uncertainty for both host nation and foreign or migrant workers. There will also be some cultural difficulties since the workers are not assimilated to their host country and are mere transients.

A possible remedy to this situation is for the host nation to identify the nationality or race of potential foreign workers whose culture most closely resembles its own to minimize potential alienation and facilitate faster acculturation; or seek foreign workers whose culture is flexible and not too different or contrary to that of the host.

The host nation can thereafter invite those foreign workers for training in the jobs they are to perform and at the same time to familiarize them with the local culture with the purpose of getting them to adapt to, and possibly adopt, local customs and attitudes. The final objective, of course, will be to make the migrant workers true immigrants who will be citizens and integral and full-fledged members of the host nation's people.

An added incentive may be the opportunity for the migrant worker to bring into the host country his family, if he or she has one, or closest relatives so that they may also enjoy the better conditions of the new land as well as stave off the worker's loneliness and homesickness.

The relatives will also be potential trainees and workers, such that, in the long run, both employers and workers will have a greater stake in maintaining and nurturing their relationship. The employers would want to keep each worker happy because the worker represents, and is part of, a group of blood-related workers. The workers would like to do their best to keep the company successful and profitable as so many of their kin depend on it for a living.

This way, the host nation will not have to continually contend with other countries in need of workers while the workers will no longer be mercenaries on a temporary sojourn but part of the community they are making a living in.

The best candidates for immigrant workers will, of course, be the unemployed citizens of the poor, undeveloped nations. Not only will the unemployed be more amenable to learning the desired job skills but they will also be more willing to work outside their homeland since there are few job opportunities where they live. The lack of opportunity will, presumably, also cause their families and relatives to be more agreeable to being transplanted in another country.

There may be some misgivings, perhaps even outright objections, to this kind of proposition from potential host nations. Japan, for instance, may not relish the possibility that the Japanese race may be diluted, that their ethnic identity may be weakened and subsumed by migrants from other lands. The fact is, Japan does not grant citizenship to workers and even long-time residents of foreign ethnic origin. But it may sooner or later have to accept the inexorable sweep of globalization.

Australia, after all, has had to abandon its "White Australia" policy almost four decades ago. The United States and other western industrialized nations have also had to periodically revise their policies and regulations vis-à-vis immigrants, both legal and illegal, not only for humanitarian considerations but also, and more importantly for those governments, for economic and political reasons, with emphasis on the former.

Japan will inevitably find its people becoming "brown" the way Americans and many erstwhile predominantly white populations have become "browned" and ethnically kaleidoscopic since the later half of the last century. Otherwise it will have to offer ever increasing compensation to transient mercenaries who feel no real allegiance or affinity towards Japan. And it will still be struggling with its problem of a shrinking ethnic population.

Perhaps Japan, and other nations that wish to preserve ethnic integrity even in this era of globalization, would do well to ponder the saga of the *Nisei* of the United States during World War II. Japanese immigrants and their offspring were confined to internment camps because of American anger and suspicions after Japan's treacherous attack on Pearl Harbor.

Many of the second generation Japanese or Nisei (children of immigrant parents) eventually served in the US military. The all-Nisei 100th Infantry Battalion and 442nd Regimental Combat Team became the most decorated US military units of the war, suffering the most number of casualties and displaying courage second to none for the flag of their adopted country.

The Nisei in World War II were shining proof that one does not have to share ethnic identity with one's countrymen to be patriots.

Dwight Eisenhower, Supreme Commander of the Allied Forces in Europe who became the 34th US president, was of German ancestry as his name indicates, and he orchestrated the decisive and final invasion of Europe that led to total defeat for Germany in that war.

If the United States did not accept immigrants, America and its allies would not have had valiant Nisei troops - nor an Eisenhower to lead them to victory. Who knows if some other general, certainly of some other ethnicity, could have succeeded as well?

Of course, that is very hypothetical, but what stands as incontrovertible fact is that an American with German blood led the world in defeating the Germans. That is history.

Where feasible, the problem of ethnic and cultural differences can be circumvented by establishing industrial plants and workplaces where the workers are already situated, as has been done by international industrial giants in the latter part of the last century. In this setup there is hardly a cultural conflict or dislocation of any sort.

But there will be many cases where it is the workers that have to be brought to the work place. Like in the staffing of hospitals, city public services, maintenance of infrastructure and operating systems that are vital to the normal survival of communities.

There may be other, better solutions to this and other problems; suffice it to say that where nations, governments and peoples are willing to adopt flexible and objective attitudes towards problems and situations, instead of being fettered by intransigent and regressive postures, solutions will be found to the greatest mutual benefit of those involved.

Nations and peoples have been building fences and walls for ages. We should tear them down, or at least open up some gates.

THE END OF POVERTY

When the world government, in conjunction with regional and local governments, has institutionalized and polished the system of providing for the needs of all people and facilitating employment and livelihood for as many of them as can be accommodated, we may consider the basic state of poverty to have been largely eliminated.

But, wait, many of the people, a vast majority of them, in fact, will still be at the bottom of the economic pyramid. Even the organized and efficient relocation of people to places and countries that need or want them would be perpetuating the system of workers migrating to rich countries, driven by poverty to do the work the citizens of such countries find too difficult or too demeaning to handle themselves. Does this mean that real poverty and the stratification of people and classes will remain in operation?

No. After the most basic human needs are assured for all citizens of the world, poverty as we know it – meaning spiritual as well as material penury - will disappear. The sharp differences in status and way of life will melt away.

Yes, physical ordeals, drudgery and lack of dignity will be things of the past that will not even be vague memories of future generations.

How will that happen?

The advances in technology have been transforming the nature of what were once rigorous and filthy and therefore undesirable tasks.

Farming is being progressively done by technicians and machines. Even collection of garbage in modern communities is no longer a stinking, disgusting affair. Trash is now collected in sanitary bags and hauled in sanitary closed trucks and the collectors wear clean uniforms and hardly have their gloved hands soiled.

Soon robots will be collecting the garbage, sweeping and vacuuming our streets, clearing up sewers, performing those tough and dirty jobs that used to be done by the poorest, most unskilled and uneducated people, or India's "untouchables."

Every human being can function and perform his tasks, whatever they may be, with a degree of dignity, as well as physical ease, and the chasms between laborers, professionals and business tycoons will no longer be that much or even significant. In fact, the time will come when robots and machines will be doing most of the work so that humans will not have to work at all, except in a few highly cerebral fields. Possibly, eventually not even that.

As to economic status, when most laborious work becomes mechanized, the workers assigned to these fields will not be lowly laborers but technicians with considerable education or specialized training. The mechanization will also allow less workers to do the work more quickly so that the budgets for their compensation will be shared by fewer individuals and, presumably, be higher on the scale. They may not be rich, but they will be neither miserable nor really poor.

Some may scoff at this hypothetical scenario, either believing it to be impossible or deeming it undesirable for human existence. Impossibility, it must be emphatically declared, is no longer a probability given the giant leaps of progress. The attainment of a state of human existence where humans no longer have to work, or do hard work, must be considered a certainty – and a most desirable goal.

Why work when you can spend your time having fun or engaging in activities you love or enjoy? Why fix your plumbing yourself when a robot can do it while you paint your own Mona Lisa or peer through a super telescope to search for a new planet?

The advance of science and technology cannot be stopped, and no one in his right mind will want to stop it. So why not reap all the blessings and conveniences from the developments that will arise from such progress?

With the international and organized management of human affairs by a world government, with various systems addressing most if not all problems in place, and technology allowing for providing basic needs and comfort and dignity for everyone, Utopia is now in sight.

This does not mean, however, that every living person will be in ecstatic bliss in his or her day-to-day existence. A person may desire a certain other to be his romantic partner and the first person's love, alas, is unrequited. Or another individual may wish to become a popular singer but either lacks talent or does not get much public acceptance. Such situations may cause unhappiness.

But those unfulfilled desires are too personal and could not possibly be provided for by any system. Unless people are willing to partake of drugs or hypnotic treatment to either help them forget their frustrations or enter a make-believe world where all their personal dreams are realized.

But then that may be a viable choice, possibly more preferable and humane compared to just allowing countless individuals to suffer lingering depression and hopelessness.

Clearly, and probably nobody can dispute the fact, the multi-pronged advances in science and technology - as well as developments in the interlinked economic situation of almost all countries - are making possible, even imperative and inevitable, the evolvement of new ways of living and functioning of individuals in their social environment and a new order in the governance of societies and communities.

In this day and age, it will be inane, even insane, for the world's leaders not to come together and work out the best possible arrangement for most, preferably all, nations, regions and peoples to cooperate for the optimum benefits that can be derived from the gathering circumstances.

As far as we can see, most problems hindering mankind from achieving universal peace, economic security and general sufficiency in basic needs are within the abilities of the present generation of leaders to confront and overcome.

The mega problems of the world economy, the environment and global warming can actually be turned into an opportunity to unite and achieve what had hitherto been thought unimaginable.

A GENTLER, KINDER WORLD

The main stumbling block to the implementation of the economic policies that will facilitate the equitable distribution of financial opportunities and material necessities is the desire of individuals, and hence the organizations they form and the nations they belong to, to accumulate and amass wealth - the old curse of acquisition.

Rich people and their business and industrial establishments will understandably resist, even sabotage, government policies and programs that may hinder or block their income-generating efforts and, worse, require them to allocate funds as contributions and not investments. Many will not willingly acquiesce to the greater good where the weal of the masses will cost them a lot of money.

Perhaps even the not-so-rich but affluent middle classes and high-income professionals will refuse to cooperate when their interests are adversely affected by certain reforms. This may lead to critical situations; for instance, doctors could go on strike or those in charge of vital public services may cut down their working hours.

It will probably be more difficult, perhaps seemingly impossible, to forgo or entirely eliminate the urge for acquisition and accumulation of material things - most importantly, money.

In his song, Lennon chose as the subject of his final verse this most fundamental and visceral urge.

"Imagine no possessions, I wonder if you can..."

In a previous chapter, we had discussed the lust for acquisition as one of the evils afflicting human society. But let us visit that subject once more and look at some other aspects of this innate desire of humans in a different context – that of its being a necessary stimulus for the survival of all humans.

In all of man's progress, this drive for acquiring, for getting to own this or that – whether a palace or a magnificent horse or a Learjet, or just a cottage by the sea – propelled man to ever greater efforts that led to the progress of civilization. For what could have motivated the Wright brothers to create a flying machine if there was nothing in it for them?

Or the pharaohs' engineers to design and build those pyramids?

True, there are also superhuman endeavors that are not propelled by material reward – artists, even when not commissioned to create something, will still paint or sculpt; the poet will write verse for its own sake, the composer will create music because it is his nature to do so. Yes, even the Wright brothers and Galileo presumably may just have wanted to advance science, or, at most, simply gain fame and honor.

But these are rare exceptions, like the missionaries who do charity work in the most poverty-stricken places of the world.

The norm of human behavior is acting and doing for compensation. The greater the effort, logically, the greater the compensation or reward.

Even without consciously wishing to amass rewards and the consequent conversion into material possessions of rewards in excess of what one can consume, a person can work and be rewarded beyond his needs and that of his family. This is very common when a person's efforts produce results that benefit many people or continuing benefits for certain clients.

Surely, he will not throw those rewards away. That will be illogical – and unnatural.

Then, too, it is very possible he may not be able to work or acquire his needs tomorrow or the day after. So he must keep what he obtained even if it is too much for this day's needs because he may need the excess tomorrow or next week.

Of course, in many parts of the world where the seasons forced man to store up for winters or periods of drought and famine, it was imperative and a matter of survival that he produce and hoard as much as he can to be able to last through the lean, unproductive months or even years.

That necessity, perhaps evolved into an urge that hardened into instinct, may be the root cause of man's developing an acquisitive nature.

Looking ahead, he will desire to amass even more reserves for the future, to ascertain that he and his family will not want in the days ahead – better yet, be assured of prosperity forever.

The escalation of the desire into greed – wanton, even rapacious, bottomless greed - could be said to be the one thing that truly separates humans from other animals. Other creatures could be afflicted with sexual urges equal to or even more powerful than we see in some humans, be as domineering and senselessly violent.

Some may at times even act with obvious compassion. But none manifest avarice.

Perhaps it is because the abstract idea of possession has not intruded into the awareness of the lower animals. Their instincts do not go beyond claiming a larger chunk of meat than they can cram into their bellies, or caching up a carcass to feed on for as long as it lasts. Or grabbing as many fruits as can be grasped with both hands and stuck inside cheek pouches.

A man, however, can have dozens of palatial mansions, more bank deposits than can be spent in profligate living by his children, grandchildren and great grandchildren, and yet still maneuver, even scheme and cheat, sometimes murder, to have more of what he already has in utter surfeit.

That is something that has to be checked, excised from the human psyche if possible – or, since that is very improbable, then let it be made a cause for shame and disgust to the extent that the acquisitive urge will have to be repressed, like the instinct to commit rape or incest.

Improbable? Impossible?

Maybe not. If the world government can institute the systems that will assure the distribution of basic needs to everyone such that no one lacks of anything a human being will require for a healthy and dignified existence and enable him to assume a proper place in society, then to possess wealth and material possessions beyond one's needs is unnecessary.

To crave and strive for riches will therefore be ridiculous and stupid at the very least; insane and evil in the extreme. Our attitudes and appreciation of life's realities will be changed, taking on new lights and meanings.

Instead of admiring and idolizing Bill Gates for his fantabulous billions that have kept him at, or near, the apex of the wealth pyramid all these years, we should admire and idolize him for the universal influence and impetus his work on computer programs and leadership in the development of cyber technology have contributed, even pioneered, for the world of today and tomorrow.

For that would be the true essence of Bill Gates, not what businesses he could afford to buy up and add to his empire, or what merciful charity he could give away through his foundation – although that is a noble and most welcome facet to his persona.

In the world we aim to build, there will be little need to amass tremendous wealth, to provide for tomorrow and a million tomorrows for one's descendants. The system will provide for everyone living and everyone to be born so long, of course, as one is willing to fill a niche in the scheme of society - which is just logical and proper.

But how do we excise the urge for acquisition and prevent it from doing the damage it has wrought on human society since the birth of civilization?

We have seen how the unfettered drive to amass wealth has resulted in misery all over the world with the periodic economic crises that beleaguered nations big and small, in the past and the most recent one that began in 2008. The economies of nations were shaken and brought down by fraudulent business practices that bloated income and asset reports which caused false appreciation of companies' financial status and stock market values, as well as by over-expansion of industries and commercial ventures fueled by careless and irresponsible desire for profit.

It will take concerted effort from leaders, institutions and ordinary individuals to spread the gospel that great wealth is not only unnecessary but the struggle to accumulate such is fraught with danger and even anathema to improving the individual and collective life of all humanity.

It can be done, I think. It must be done, I am sure.

Alright, then. But what about the rich people? The business tycoons, the moguls of industry, the bigwigs of banking and finance? Are they then to stop making money and abandon the enterprises or let them grind to a complete halt? What about the highly-paid professionals in different fields, must they quit and retire from their occupations?

Wouldn't that bring about a total breakdown of the economic system? Where will workers work if industrial and commercial establishments stopped operating? Who will be doing anything? Can government just take over everything?

No, not at all. No to all that.

First, government, whether of the world or regional and local jurisdictions, cannot hope to equal private managers and business owners in expertise and dedication to their respective fields. Second, and more importantly, there is no reason any industrial or commercial concern should close shop even if it becomes widely accepted that excessive profit-making is not an honorable goal.

They can, and should, continue performing their roles in the scheme of things, strive for further excellence and progress, even if – or because – that will lead to accumulation of more wealth.

Hey! Isn't that where we were in the first place? And isn't that what we are trying to change?

Well, we must acknowledge the inescapable truth that there are some things we cannot change. We cannot expunge the instinct for survival, whether in man or beast. We also cannot ask people to work for nothing.

Therefore, we should let people go on doing what they do best - work for material reward.

Oh, but with a difference. We can place a cap on their total income. Beyond a certain point, a man or a woman can no longer earn financial rewards. Most nations already have a system of taxation based on income brackets, whereby the larger the income is, the larger the percentage of tax that must be paid. A system whereby people and corporations can only make a certain amount of money every year will be just a modification of the income bracket tax scheme.

Of course, governments will have to institute safeguards against cheating and disguising income as well as expenditures, perhaps formulate stringent auditing rules. The system of cashless transactions is of additional relevance here as all fund transfers will be on record and can be traced.

What about investing huge amounts, say billions, to invent new products or blaze new trails? Only the prospect of huge profits motivates super rich individuals and giant corporations to fund research and development – to make a revolutionary car engine, a cure for all sorts of cancer, even perhaps a solar-powered spaceship for mining expeditions to Mars. Will they risk vast resources on ventures that could not, and would not - by force of law and official government policy - give them commensurate returns if and when such are successful?

The best economic and financial minds of the world can surely formulate ways to facilitate due rewards for such ventures. Profits emanating from development of new products and technology may be exempted from existing income limits of the institutions and the individual stockholders; surely ways can be thought up to keep the wheels of progress rolling.

After establishing the just and practical limitations to individual and institutional income, excess earnings will either be expropriated by the government or, to provide an incentive to the income earner, be disposed according to a person's, or an institution's, preference.

The field of choices for the disposal of the excess income must, however, be confined to causes that will benefit society and humanity.

The super rich can be allowed to use their surplus money to show how successful they are, in other words, they still earn bragging rights. However, instead of a new luxury yacht, Tiger Woods can show off a fenced-off section of Brazilian jungle he has bought as a nature preserve with the sign "A Gift From Tiger Woods to All People of the World."

Or, rather than do something stupendous like chartering a Boeing 747 to pick up guests from around the world to celebrate his birthday, the Sultan of Brunei can put up a center for the rehabilitation of widows and orphans on both sides of the hostilities in Afghanistan.

Would the big moneymakers strive to attain success and keep making money just so they can do good deeds?

As we have seen, the rich cannot sit on their laurels, or their blue chip piles. If super-giant General Motors and behemoth Lehman Brothers could suddenly come crashing down, no establishment is fail-safe and rock-solid. The major stockholders and management hierarchy of every industrial and commercial institution have to be alert and on their toes year in and year out – even day in and day out.

Remember, too, that the competition will be burning the midnight oil to beat everyone in the field. There will always be those that do not yet make the maximum allowable income who will be straining to reach that plateau. Yes, tycoons, super executives and financial whizzes have to fight tooth and nail even if only to stay where they are and as they are.

They may be convinced not to want too much or too much more, but they sure as hell would not accede to losing what they already have. So, they won't be giving up the struggle anytime soon.

Then if they are too successful, the rest of society can help unburden them.

Now, the fact that they cannot keep all their booty will most probably restrain them from going for overkill, particularly not to the extent of employing unscrupulous and foul means. That will facilitate and encourage fair and honest competition. Why should businessmen and corporate executives risk prosecution if they cannot keep the loot anyway?

Then, perhaps, probably, hopefully, we can see a more rational, and less materialistic, channeling of capital and effort in most, if not all, of human endeavor.

No, Donald Trump. You don't have to make several million dollars today and a few more tomorrow. You may not have to make another dollar. Your children and grandchildren will still have food on the table. And they will get to attend school. Even if you die tonight and orphan them tomorrow.

Sure, you can still build another fabulous hotel tower here and there, but not because of the fortunes they will earn but as edifices to your energy and vision. So you can beat your chest on the rooftop and feel immense pride at your achievements. We will not begrudge you that. We will even praise and thank you for the hydroponics farms you will establish in Botswana so that people there will not have to battle with wild elephants to protect their crops in the wide open veldt.

Yes, huge personal riches will be both meaningless and a mark of decadence and nonconformity with the true spirit of human society. For surely, inevitably, we will be able to make people realize that there are those who have so little or none at all because others, some very few others, have too much – way too much. And that the world we are building will ensure that everyone will have enough – for the world government, the Big Brother of the New Order, will see to that.

We shall spread the word and instill in the mind of every human being that the world's bounty is meant to be distributed, not hoarded, that focusing too much on the needs of the future prevents us from enjoying the blessings of today.

No one has to grab much more than he needs if no one else is trying to grab it away first, or at all. Big Brother will also see to it that nobody grabs too much, anyway.

No need for greed or hunger.

"Imagine all the people sharing all the world."

"Sir Thomas More X" is the pen name of Enrique De Jesus, a writer from the Philippines whose previous work includes fiction and non-fiction, articles and essays, sports columns and movie screenplays, in both English and his native Filipino.

This is his first English book.

www.ingramcontent.com/pod-product-compliance
Lightning Source LLC
Chambersburg PA
CBHW062053270326
41931CB00013B/3058